THE HILL OF HOPE

This is the second of two fascinating books illuminating the life of Jesus by Ken Hornsby.

His first job was in a public library, which he put to good use by writing *Is that the Library speaking?* an amused look at the foibles of the library system and the people who use it. He then moved on to become an advertising copy and script writer, latterly as a creative director in a multi-national advertising agency and then starting his own consultancy. During this time he wrote *The Padded Sell,* a wry look at the advertising industry. He has also published a novel which was shortlisted for The Guardian junior fiction prize; a remembrance of his experiences in the war; and had two plays performed publicly.

His companion book on the birth of Jesus, *The House of Bread,* was published in 2006.

BY THE SAME AUTHOR

Is that the Library speaking?
The Padded Sell
Wet Behind the Ears
A Child at War
The House of Bread

PLAYS

Don't Mind Me
The Waiting Room

THE HILL
OF HOPE

THE HILL
OF HOPE

THE FULL STORY OF THE TRIAL, DEATH
AND RESURRECTION OF JESUS

KEN HORNSBY

Published by FreeHand Publishing Limited
175 Munster Road, London, SW6 6DA
Registered Office Centurion House, 37 Jewry Street, London, EC3N 2ER

First published 2007

A catalogue record for this book is available from the British Library

ISBN: 978-0-9551847-4-1

Design and production John Nicholls
Typeset in Bembo
Printed and bound in Great Britain by
William Clowes Ltd, Beccles, Suffolk

To my daughters Jill and Ruth with love

PREFACE

The Bible can be hard to read. The language is beautiful but it is old-fashioned, with words that are not in common usage today and sentence construction that can be difficult to comprehend.

Furthermore, the greatest stories within are told differently by the various writers, sometimes with events transposed, sometimes with timelines that do not seem to make sense, sometimes with quite contradictory narratives.

As a result it is not read as much as it deserves to be, and the two great events – the birth and the death of Jesus – are known by most people only in outline. Then again, the Bible is often sparse with detail, covering little of the background and leaving the reader to complete the gaps for himself. The birth of Jesus, for example, appears in only two of the Gospels, and takes up no more than half a page of print. The previous companion book to this, *The House of Bread,* extends the Christmas story to full length, filling in the historical and sociological background.

Similarly, in *The Hill of Hope,* I have set out to take the trial, crucifixion and death of Jesus as described by the first four Gospels of the New Testament and re-present it readably, accessible to all. It is the most extraordinary story ever documented, immense in its implications, bursting with contradictions and unexplained detail.

It is not made any more comprehensible because there are a number of fundamental differences between the first three Gospels on the one hand – those according to Matthew, Mark and Luke (the so-called 'synoptic' gospels – from the Greek *sunoptikes* and meaning a commonly agreed survey) and that from John on the other. Mark is generally believed to be the first to have been written (something like 70 years after the death of Jesus) and John the last (120 to 150 years afterwards). Obviously none of them had first-hand knowledge; thus no-one can be sure precisely what happened.

The only thing historians do agree on is that the whole thing doesn't fully add up, particularly as written by the Synoptics. But then it was never really meant to be 'history'. The authors were early Christians writing in a period when there was an anti-Jewish momentum developing, and at least part of their agenda was to show the Jews in a poor light. Further, another part of their agenda was to write their stories so as to match earlier prophecies. Thus the cart frequently come before the horse.

But my purpose is not to explain or challenge the Gospels. Many scholars have done that at length with varying answers. I have just taken the Bible story as presented and, hopefully, illuminated and clarified it. Where the inconsistencies between the Synoptics and John were too great to be mutually inclusive I have simply made my own decisions.

Even with its inconsistencies it is an amazing story: partly a whodunnit, partly a whydunnit, always entirely engrossing.

KH

CONTENTS

Preface

CHAPTER 1

THE DARK CLOUDS GATHER

They had heard the stories. The withered hand that was cured, the cripples who rose from their beds and walked, the leper who touched him and was healed.

And when they heard he was there, only a few miles away, they started to come together. The news was spreading: "Jesus is coming, the man who heals is coming, the man who is going to save us is coming." The tiny bunches of people became small crowds, lone individuals linked with others, all made their way across the scrub land at the bottom of the hills of Galilee. Together they climbed up towards where they could see the bigger crowd accumulating.

The noise was growing too. For these were not all peaceable people. The men in particular numbered warriors, zealots, gang leaders and preachers among them. Many were desperate. Desperate for someone to champion them, to rise up against the Romans, to restore the Jews to their rightful place of independence and rescue them from their enforced allegiance to the Romans, the hated occupiers and law-makers. They were desperate for the leader who they knew would one day come. They were desperate for this Jesus to be the Messiah, the leader, the deliverer. From what they had heard this man was their best chance, their best hope.

Still they were gathering. Three thousand, four thousand, perhaps even five thousand. Those arriving last could barely see the man at the top; or the men, for there seemed to be two or three who were conferring together, their robes blowing wildly in the strong wind at the top of the hill. It was cold too, only April, and near the time of the Passover. Yet the excitement of the crowd was enough to overcome the elements. Men were shouting, raising their staffs, encouraging each other. The women, always quieter, were mostly sitting, hoping to be uplifted by the words of this likely leader whose fame was slowly spreading out from Nazareth, the town where he was thought to have been born and grown up and where he had started his preaching.

What they didn't know was that he was already beginning to fall

1

out with his family there and exasperate those closest to him. They wouldn't have known that this was simply due to the strength of his beliefs, so strong and so reactionary that his family couldn't always stomach them. Like any man who was individual and strong enough to hew his own path he upset many people who preferred a quieter or more conformist life. And his family were no different from many in finding his ways too hard to deal with.

But this was just what the more questioning Jews needed now, a man who was powerful enough and determined enough to flout the authorities, both Jewish and Roman, and go his own way. Which they very much hoped was their way too.

At the top of the hill there was a conversation. It seemed simple enough, but in reality it was a test.

Jesus looked down over the noisy crowd and said to Philip next to him, "It's nearly Passover. Look at all these people. They're hungry. Where on earth can we buy bread for them all? They've come to support us; we owe them food at least."

It was a question Philip hadn't expected. But then he frequently didn't expect either the questions or the answers he got from Jesus. He tried to think, and failed. "There are so many," he said hopelessly. "You'd have to spend a fortune to provide something for everyone. And even that wouldn't be enough really to feed them. There's nothing we can do."

Jesus looked silently back. Philip was already failing.

But another had half an idea. Andrew spoke up. "There is a lad here. He's got five barley loaves and two small fishes. Not that that's going to go very far. But I suppose it's a start." He looked at Jesus, hoping to have pleased him a little.

Jesus looked at the pair of them. Not for the first time they had disappointed him. And they would do so many times more in the time that was to come. Especially at the last, as he already knew at the back of his mind.

He looked from them down the hill to the multitude standing about, still shouting.

"Make them sit down. Make the *men* sit down," he said quietly. "Concentrate on the men. Quieten them down, make them sit. This is not a battle rally, whatever they think"

Assuming there was no answer to the problem of the food, the disciples left the top of the hill and started getting the men to sit. It was not easy, calming an excitable crowd looking for inspiration for war. But as Philip, Andrew, Simon Peter and a few others moved through the crowd the men gradually sank to the grass and quietened down, joining the women in small groups and reducing their shouts to a quieter chattering.

When they had all settled, Jesus took the five loaves and two fishes, gave thanks, and distributed some to those nearest to him. Now quiet and seated, the others lower down the slopes saw what he was doing. Some of them rooted around in their bags and found something they could eat themselves. Some had fruit, some small loaves, some had even prepared and brought a small meal with them in readiness for the Passover. Those that had, ate. Then they noticed that some of those nearby had nothing, so in the quiet that was now settling over the crowd, they offered a little to their neighbours. Soon everyone was eating something. The five thousand were fed.

And after they were fed, Jesus said, "Gather up whatever's left, so nothing is wasted". They gathered, and found they had gathered no less than twelve basketfuls.

Then Jesus repeated Philip's words to him: "There's nothing we can do? To feed them?"

Philip looked embarrassed. "It was a good trick master, I hadn't thought of that."

"A trick?"

"Well, a good idea then. Guessing they would share once they'd calmed down and sat. Everyone's happy now. We can get on - *you* can get on - and preach."

"Aren't you missing something?" asked Jesus.

Philip looked puzzled. "I can't think of anything."

"What have we got here? What has happened?"

Philip faltered and could provide no answer. Jesus looked at him and found himself thinking back. It was not the first time those nearest had failed to understand. He remembered when he had first started to gather his little group of disciples, those who already believed in him and thought the best of him.

But that was not how everyone had been. Not even his own

3

family had been behind him then. Not even his mother. Some of his friends and relations had thought him mad. The stories of his healings, of his mixing with those who were outcasts, or caring for those who others would leave alone, had caused some bitter comments.

"He is beside himself."

"He is mad, to consort with these people."

"He must be restrained."

And then even more pointed remarks from those not willing to believe all they were told, or putting the worst complexion on it.

"Where does he get all this? What is all this wisdom that he claims? And all these miracles he is supposed to be doing? He's only the carpenter, Mary's son. His brothers James, Joses, Judah and Simon and his sisters all live here with us. We're all just ordinary people. Who does he think he is?"

As response and in a moment of pure irony, Jesus had said, "No prophet goes unhonoured. Except of course among his own people and in his own land and in his own home." And continuing the irony he laid hands on some sick people who immediately began to show signs of improvement. On his face the look that said, "Can you *still* not believe?"

But then the moment of no return. In a last attempt to claim him back from his extreme views, his mother and brothers came to see him. They stood outside the house where he was staying. A small crowd had gathered and they couldn't get through.

They sent a messenger in. "Your mother and family want to talk to you."

But it was too late. They had misunderstood him and disappointed him. They had thought him possessed of absurd and dangerous ideas. They were not with him. And being him, he did not let it pass. He appeared at the door and spoke to his followers.

"Who *is* my mother? Who *are* my brothers? I say to you, *you are my family*. Whoever does the will of God, *these* are my family."

Always ready to speak his mind he was prepared to put away even his own family from him if they did not follow. And he would tell the world too. From that day he had been estranged from his family; just one of the reasons why he had left the region of his birth.

"Aren't you missing something?" said Jesus to Philip again, "What do you think is happening here?"

Philip could think of nothing original to say. "We've found food for the crowd? They're fed?"

"Not enough," said Jesus, "you can do better than that. *What has happened here?*"

Philip looked at the other disciples and slowly they recounted exactly what they had seen happen. "We quietened the men down, they sat amongst themselves, they talked, they found enough food among them to feed them all. What else, master?"

"You have said it. They quietened, they spoke, they were fulfilled. Do you not see this is how we should all be? Our world is full of fighting people, people who want to raise war against each other, people who exclude those they think aren't worthy, people who think they are the only ones who count."

And then Jesus became more intense. Those around him sensed he was telling them something vital; they stared hard, and listened.

"*This is our mission.* We must get all men talking to each other, forgetting their differences, their individual beliefs and ambitions. We must stop them being political terrorists. Instead they must all face forwards and be of one mind. Otherwise there are terrible dangers ahead for the Jewish people. Only then will the wars cease – but far more important – only then will we be ready for the Kingdom of God. We have not just fed five thousand people here; we have seen that if we share and are of one mind there is room for all in the Kingdom of Heaven."

It was an amazing success.

But it was also the beginning of the end.

For the idea spread through the crowd that another miracle had been done and to Jesus's dismay they began to view him as a king come to lead them. "This really is that prophet who we knew would one day come into this world," they were saying. They had not taken his real message into their hearts, but instead once again had seen what they wanted to see.

He alone knew that to proceed in this direction would end in tragedy. It was never in his mind to be a warring leader; as he had said, the answer to their difficulties lay in talking and debating, not marching with weapons. In an attempt to calm the situation down he took himself away alone into the hills.

But the damage was already being done. The stories of his views and his attitudes were already spreading. It was hard to tell who was most annoyed by him, the Romans or his own kinsmen, the Jews themselves.

The Jewish Scribes and the Pharisees muttered among themselves. The Scribes were doctors of law, living mostly in Jerusalem. They too had disciples gathered around them; it was their task and duty to decide on the interpretation of the Jewish law and the ways to carry it out. This was a vital job, since as time passed by the original Hebrew laws were less read and even less understood. The Scribes were the living embodiment of Jewish law. They were not officers and not priests; they were not paid either, and most had other jobs. But they were important. Already beginning to replace the age-old Jewish aristocracy, they had a position of great power. And they were not about to allow it to be undermined by a peasant from Nazareth who was saying things they couldn't agree with and gathering a crowd of devoted followers about him.

Grouped with the Scribes were the Pharisees. Their name is derived from a word meaning "separated" – detached from anything unclean or sinful. As a group of people they were established well over a hundred years previously and were the most determined and dedicated sector of all the Jewish race. They were not a violent people; they much preferred to submit quietly to their law and wanted all other Jews to do the same. But they were fervent leaders of prayer, with a deep following in the synagogues. Together with the Scribes they were the leaders of the Jews. Like the Scribes they were becoming deeply troubled by the emergence of Jesus as a different sort of leader who was preaching quite different rules. And in particular they could not come to terms with his views on the forgiveness of sinners.

A meeting was being held.

Benjamin asked, "Have you heard what he has called us?"

There were a dozen in the room, some Pharisees, some Scribes.

They exchanged glances; they had an idea what was coming.

"What this time?" asked Judah wearily.

"Snakes and vipers."

The glances became frozen. The language was getting stronger; almost as if Jesus wanted to confront them in public.

"And why?" Samuel didn't want an answer but felt they should all have it.

"Why? Why? Because he seems to feel the need to insult us," said Benjamin, his jaw working furiously. "On one hand he says people should listen to us and hear what we say – and on the other hand that they should not follow us or our works."

"So he wants it both ways," said Judah from his seat in the corner. "Give a show of agreeing with us, then encourage his people to go against us."

"You should hear what else he has been saying." Benjamin was working himself up into a fury. It was not like him and the others watched him intently. "He says we give burdens to others to carry but never help others ourselves."

"Do you know what I heard?" asked another of the Pharisees. "Some of the people are saying he gets his power from the devil. Really. Apparently there was a man who had lost his voice, and this Jesus healed him and made the voice return. Just like that. Of course, I don't really believe it. He has got a way with him, there's no doubt about that. And I suppose it's possible he could in some way hypnotise someone into getting his voice back. But the point is – people were beginning to say that if he gets his power from the devil, perhaps he is the devil. And then going about preaching in the name of the Jews. We cannot possibly allow that."

Another of the Scribes spoke up.

"Yes, I've heard that story too. But he did have a good answer to it, to be fair. He said it didn't make any sense, that accusation. If the devil had given him the power to cast out demons, the devil would be fighting against himself, casting out the devil's own demons."

"Yes, well, he's very clever when it comes to words. That's what makes him so dangerous."

Absolam, a Pharisee, had another story to tell. "I have a cousin, a Pharisee who lives over towards Galilee. He invited Jesus to

7

dinner. They had a bit of a set to, I can tell you. It started when Jesus sat down at the table without the usual ritual washing of hands. My cousin started to say something about it but it was like he had set a tiger loose. Instead of apologising and washing his hands, Jesus turned on him. 'That's the trouble with you Pharisees. You take all the trouble in the world to clean the outside of the cup or the dish, but inside you are filthy – full of greed and wickedness.' Well, you can imagine what my cousin thought of that."

Benjamin almost choked. "Then it's even worse than I thought. But what did he mean by it? Did he give any explanation for his outburst?"

"Well, sort of, " said Absolam, "not that it made things much better. He claimed we love the best seats in the synagogue and the respect we get from others and then don't support the poor like we ought. And then another insult – he said we were like hidden graves in a field. People walked over us without realising what corruption they were stepping on."

"What on earth did your cousin do?"

"Well he started to object, as you might think, but he didn't get very far for Jesus came right out with a final insult. 'You and the Scribes – you hide the key of knowledge. You don't enter the Kingdom of God yourself and you prevent others from entering'. It was a terrible evening. They tried to get him to incriminate himself with a lot of tough questions, but of course he was quite careful, not admitting to anything you could do anything about, just being argumentative. As you say, he's very clever with words."

"He may be clever with words," said Benjamin, "but if he goes on like this it won't be just we Jews who will be against him. He's only got to make a few more remarks about being the real leader and he'll get that heroic governor Herod Antipas and all his Romans on his trail too. I'm beginning to think he's got a bit of a death wish."

And then another meeting. This time it was the Sadducees. Not unlike the Pharisees in their beliefs, the Sadducees were an upper class priestly sect who had their base in the Temple and met there frequently to discuss and guide the Jews in their faith.

Bartholomew spoke up. "I take it we all know what he is saying these days."

Saul: "He is going directly against our teaching."

And Boaz: "He is not speaking for *me*."

Bartholomew again: "He is using stories that on the face of it make sense, to preach precisely the opposite of what we believe. Have you heard the one about the son who left his family, only to be rewarded when he came back?"

Not all of them were quite so ready to criticise. One, keeping his face down under his veil, nevertheless spoke up bravely. "But what is he really saying? Isn't he making a valid point?"

"All right," said Bartholomew, "let's examine the story. This is what he says. A rich man has two sons. One, the older, works hard in the fields for him. The other, a bit of a wastrel, asks his father for his inheritance now, rather than having to wait till his death. The father, being a reasonable man, if over-indulgent, agrees and gives the younger son the money. But what does he do? Work hard to thank his father? Oh no, he just goes off to have a good time, spends – and wastes – all his money, and finds himself starving. He takes a job as a pig man and even the pig food looks good to him. Then one day he wakes up and thinks, "Even my father's servants are better off than me. Perhaps I should go home again.

"So he goes home. And his father is thrilled to see him, brings out the finest clothes, prepares a great welcome-back banquet. But the older son, who has taken no money and continued to work hard on his father's behalf, gets really annoyed by this. 'Is this fair?' he asks. His father replies, 'Your brother was dead and is found. Of course we rejoice'."

"And the point is?" asked Boaz.

"The point is, according to Jesus, sinners should be welcomed just as much as non-sinners. According to Jesus, *everyone* should be entitled to go to heaven, not just those who have followed God's word. In fact he's going even further than that. It's the sinners who repent that God cares most about. Doesn't matter whether they're adulterers, thieves, torturers, swindlers. If they're really sorry, they should be admitted to heaven. Listen, these are his very words which I heard from a cousin who was there: 'Heaven will be happier over one lost sinner who returns to God than over ninety-nine others who are righteous and haven't strayed away'."

"It's not right," said Saul. "If there's no reward for following God's laws, there's no sense in it at all. We just can't have this sort of talk going about. "

The man beneath the veil kept quiet. Jesus's views made a sort of uncomfortable sense to him, but he was not going to stand against the others.

And yet another meeting
The Scribes were up in arms.
"He is not being respectful to the Sabbath."
"He is working on the Sabbath."
"He said the Sabbath was made for man, not man for the Sabbath."

What had he done this time? He had indeed worked on the Sabbath, if you can call healing someone working. He was in the synagogue, teaching as usual. Out of the corner of his eye he caught sight of an old woman bent almost double. She had been crippled for nearly twenty years.

Stopping his teaching for a moment for something he considered even more important, he called her over. Fixing her with those deep and piercing eyes that seemed to be able to work miracles, he said, "Woman, you are healed of your sickness".

She looked back up to him and was caught in the brilliance of his gaze, was almost hypnotised by the strength of will shining out from them. She suddenly felt that everything was possible if you believed, that mere day-to-day problems were of no account compared with true belief in God, that He could overcome everything.

Still caught by his eyes she felt herself casting the problems of her body off and slowly found she was standing more and more upright, until she stood as she had not stood for as long as she could remember. Was this a miracle - or simply the triumph of belief? She didn't know and didn't care, for one way or another this was God answering her prayers and she gave her own thanks back praising him for his great goodness.

But there were those there who were horrified.

The Chief Rabbi was shocked that Jesus had caused her to be healed on the Sabbath and he addressed the crowd over Jesus's head.

"There are six days for working," he called. "If you want to be healed, come on those days, not on the Sabbath."

But Jesus was not to be ignored or talked over. In one of those replies guaranteed to cause more controversy, he fixed the Rabbi with a piercing look and did not mince his words.

"You hypocrite," he said, "aren't you working here today? Don't you untie your ass from its stall and take it to water?"

The Rabbi had no answer to this. But Jesus had not finished. "Satan has held this poor woman in his hands for eighteen years. Why should I give him even one more day to have power over her? Which is more important – the Sabbath or getting this woman back from evil?"

There was a mixed reaction from those in the synagogue who had heard and seen all this. Some of the older ones still couldn't take the idea that priorities weren't necessarily what they always had thought them to be. Others understood the point and nodded thoughtfully. Yet others spoke up loudly in favour of Jesus. But the Scribes and the Pharisees and the Rabbi kept quiet. For their power and their authority was being threatened. They kept silent and bided their time. One day they would stop this dangerous man who was undermining so much of what they stood for.

Of course Jesus knew he was stirring up trouble. Indeed some of his followers were beginning to feel it was deliberate and it worried them. Some even started to drift away, not wanting to be associated with the difficulties they sensed were to come. Some found his words too harsh, even though they could see the arguments behind them. Some just felt he was overstepping the mark and claiming too much for himself.

Both the Pharisees and Jesus's followers had heard his remarks about the forgiveness of sins. John the Baptist had already said that baptism was a token of forgiveness of sins and his followers were happy enough to accept that rather academic argument. But then one day Jesus went much farther. Usually he kept his own words on a tight rein. Always ready to be outspoken, at the same time he was careful not to incriminate himself. Until one day he said that he himself had the power to forgive sins.

And now the leaders of the Jews were really upset. For only God could forgive sins. There was only one God and he was certainly not a wayward preacher from over the hills.

Yet even this was not the most damaging thing he had to say. The next nearly had him stoned to death.

He was in the temple and some of the elders were goading him. They knew he meant trouble for them and they were desperate for him to incriminate himself so they could move against him without taking the risk of upsetting his many followers.

"So when are you going to tell us?" they asked innocently. "Don't keep us in suspense, come out with it and tell us you are the Messiah."

Perhaps he was getting tired. Perhaps he was beginning to feel it was time to push forward in his work. Perhaps he knew the end for him was near and that now was the moment to stop prevaricating.

"I have already told you," he replied. "You can see that what I do is done in the name of my father. But you don't want to see it, do you? Because you are not part of my flock. My flock are safe; I give them eternal life and they will never perish because my father has given them to me. No-one can take them away. Because my father and I are one."

My father and I are one. He had said it, in public. He was the same as God. To the Scribes, Pharisees and Sadducees this was simple blasphemy. They picked up stones to throw at him. He left quickly, but not before adding, "... if I do my father's work you will realise he is in me and I in him".

From then on he was doomed, both by the Jews and the Romans.

The first step was being forced to leave Peraea where John the Baptist had centred his preaching.

Herod Antipas, ruler of that territory and son of Herod the Great who had tried to kill Jesus at birth, had already just had John the Baptist put to death. It was an edgy area, wild and rocky, perfect for guerrilla warfare and general military mayhem. Antipas had been well aware that John the Baptist had been attracting vast crowds. And vast crowds were fertile feeding grounds for treason. The Baptist had been preaching that earthly kingdoms would be supplanted by the Kingdom of God; not what an insecure ruler wanted to hear.

There was another thing. And this time it was personal. The Baptist had been criticising Antipas in public for his rather complicated private life. So first Antipas imprisoned the Baptist for preaching against him; then decided he was becoming a serious threat and had him executed. And Antipas was well aware of the bond between Jesus and John the Baptist and so was on the lookout for trouble.

Jesus therefore decided Peraea was too dangerous and returned to Galilee, perhaps a strange decision, since Galilee was also under Antipas's rule. What Jesus might not have known was that Antipas was being told that he was another John the Baptist, with similar views on marriage, divorce and leadership. Someone had even told Antipas that Jesus was The Baptist reborn.

So now Jesus had two sets of enemies in Galilee. The Scribes, Pharisees and Sadducees, devout Jews whom he had challenged so robustly - and the Herodians, landowners, aristocrats and supporters of Antipas who had no wish for an awkward Jew to be stirring up public unrest.

Then Jesus managed to inflame the position even further. One of his early followers, Joanna the wife of one of Antipas's stewards called Chuza, heard that Antipas was interested in meeting him. Finding this hard to believe, Jesus made his feelings about this idea publicly plain: he had no desire whatever to meet Antipas. The situation thus deteriorated.

But Antipas was loath to capture Jesus and put him to death, not wishing to risk further discontent by repeating John the Baptist's execution. So in an unusual moment of solidarity with the Jews, he encouraged the Pharisees to persuade Jesus to remove himself from the area.

These Jews, already thinking along the same lines for their own reasons, needed little encouragement. Jesus departed for Bethsaida across the Sea of Galilee and outside Antipas's fiefdom.

But he didn't stay for long. He decided his time was come and set off on the seventy mile journey to Jerusalem. The Kingdom of God was at hand. And so was his last week on this earth.

CHAPTER 2

A BOILING CITY

The disciples said it was a bad idea. "You shouldn't go to Jerusalem. You know Herod Antipas is against you. It is too dangerous. They'll stone you."

But Jesus had a second reason for going south towards Jerusalem. His great friend Lazarus, who lived just a few miles outside Jerusalem in a small town called Bethany, was seriously ill and on the verge of death. His two sisters, Mary and Martha, had got a message to Jesus and Jesus was determined to see his old friend. In fact, he was determined to do more than just see him.

But the disciples' pleas were serious. They knew Jesus was in desperate danger going to Jerusalem and they did all they could to stop him.

But, as ever, he had an answer. "We have two choices. We can walk in the daylight – or in the darkness. If we go in the day we'll be in no trouble, for we can see what we are doing. If we go in the dark we'll stumble. Let us walk in the light."

The disciples were not convinced. They were used to his stories, the way he always likened one thing to another, and realised when he said "Walk in the light" he meant walk in the light cast by God. But this was too easy; they feared he did not see the real danger he was in. And in any case they were not as brave or as believing as Jesus and were sure he was going into danger. But his mind was made up.

Nevertheless he waited two days before setting off.

The disciples worried. They didn't want him to go, but if he was, they did not want to waste time. "Shouldn't we hurry if we are going? Won't it be too late for Lazarus?"

Jesus said, "His sickness will not lead to death. That is not the nature of his illness. His sickness is for one reason only: for the glory of God. And as a result the Son of God will be glorified too."

They didn't like this. As before some of them felt that Jesus was putting himself up too high. Many sympathised with the Jewish priests who believed God was one and indivisible and that it was blasphemy to say otherwise. Some even found themselves in agreement with the Romans who were wondering whether he was not about to bring civil war to the country by claiming such leadership. Others were just frightened by the way everything was escalating. As so often the disciples disappointed him by their lack of faith. Jesus knew the situation was escalating, but this was his plan.

Then he had something new to say. "Our friend Lazareth is sleeping. But I am going to wake him up."

"But isn't sleeping good? Doesn't the fact that he is able to sleep suggest perhaps he is getting better? Shouldn't we leave him to sleep and recover, rather than disturb him?"

Jesus said, "You haven't understood me. Let me be plain. When I use the word asleep I mean dead. Lazarus is dead – to this world. But it is good we weren't there at the time of his death, because what will happen now will help you believe in me. Come; we shall go to see him – and you will see too."

So they made their way to Bethany, but when they arrived they discovered that Lazarus had already been lying in his grave for four days. Many of the Jews from Jerusalem who knew the family had gathered at the house to comfort them, but when Martha heard that Jesus was coming she could not wait but rushed out to meet him before he got to the house. Upset that he had not come earlier, she should could not hold her emotion back and cried out, "If you had come before, my brother would not have died. But even now it is not too late, because I know whatever you ask of God he will grant it".

Jesus tried to calm her. "Your brother will rise again."

"Oh I know he will rise again at the judgment day. But I want him alive *now.*"

Jesus fixed her with that look of his that seemed to blot everything else out except what he was saying and doing. As so often, and like so many other people, Martha found herself believing every word; every doubt banished.

His eyes boring into her, she found herself overwhelmed by the strength of his personality. He said, "I am the resurrection. I am the life. He who believes in me, even if he were dead, shall live again. Anyone who believes in me shall never die. Do you believe in what I say?"

Transfixed by his look and his words, Martha could only say, "Yes, Lord". And then, such was the power she felt coming from him, she found herself declaring, "I believe you are the Christ, the Son of God, who has come into the world". The words spoken, she felt overcome and rushed away, back to her sister Mary, leaving Jesus and the disciples where they were.

Jesus called after her, "Send Mary out to me".

She heard the words and back at the house, she slipped in and quietly said to Mary, "The Master has come and is asking for you."

Mary quickly stood up and hurried out. The others, who had been comforting her, thought she was going to the grave and followed her. But she outstripped them and when she found Jesus, said – like her sister had – "If you had been here my brother would not have died".

She was in tears and the others, now caught up with here, were in tears also.

Jesus asked, in tears for the sadness of the sisters, "Where have you laid him?"

"Come and see."

The crowd of Jews, seeing Jesus also crying, said among themselves, "See how he loved Lazarus".

But not everyone was so charitable. In one conversation they were saying, "Since this Jesus had made blind men see again, couldn't he have saved Lazarus from dying?"

Whether or not Jesus heard this was not clear. It was impossible to tell if this had made him more determined than ever to prove himself. But he marched on with the sisters, the crowd following until they reached the place where Lazarus was laid in a cave with a stone across the front of it.

He said, "Take away the stone".

But Martha replied, "He has been dead for four days. The smell of death will be terrible."

Jesus looked her and said sternly, "Did I not say if you believe you will see God's glory?"

So Martha and Mary and one of the others managed to roll the heavy stone away.

Jesus then prayed out loud: "Father, I thank you for hearing me.

I know you always hear me, but now that the people here have listened to me they will see that you have really sent me here."

Then he called out loudly, "Lazarus. Come forth".

Was what happened next a true miracle? Or was it once again the strength of Jesus's personality that had broken through a sick man's coma and revived him? Had Lazarus really been dead? Or had he so nearly slipped away and breathed so faintly that his family thought him dead?

At that moment it was unimportant. For to everyone's amazement and excitement Lazarus slowly moved forward out of the cave, his hands and feet still bound with the grave clothes, a napkin still around his head.

"Free him from the clothes so he may go," said Jesus, dropping to his feet and giving thanks – as so many of the others were doing. But not all.

Some were not willing to believe what Jesus had said and thought it all a trick. Quietly they melted away and went back to their friends, the Pharisees, and told them what had happened.

Others, but not those who were there at the time and had seen it for themselves, decided this whole story was a metaphor; a story that was more symbol than truth. That Lazarus's "death" was not death at all, but just an example of a man who had become deaf to the teachings of Jesus. What Jesus had done in reviving him was no more than reviving his faith. It was one of those stories that got about and not to be taken at face value. It was just a story.

But those who were there were never to be persuaded that they had seen anything other than a miracle where Jesus had reawakened life in a man who had died days earlier.

And it was too big a story to be ignored. A meeting was quickly called, a council of Pharisees and Chief Priests.

"We must take action," said one of the leaders. "These miracles, if that is what they are, that this man does: this will mean huge trouble for us, for he is gathering a multitude of followers who think like him and are not of the true faith."

"It's worse than that," said another. "If his following becomes so big and so strong the Romans are going to get extremely worried…"

"…and you can guess what they'll do," said yet another. "They'll put us right down. They'll destroy not just our position here, they'll destroy the whole Jewish nation."

The man who held the position of the chief High Priest that year, Caiaphas, then spoke words that would reverberate through the centuries to come. Although he did not know it at the time, they were words that altered history.

"I think we should consider that one man should die for the nation, rather than the nation should die for one man".

And from that moment, the Jews started to conspire to put Jesus to death.

It was now the week before Passover, and Jesus stayed on in Bethany after the raising of Lazarus.

By Jewish rules the Passover meal had to be eaten within the walls of the holy city; anyone who tried to do so beyond the boundary could be punished by a beating of forty strokes. As a result the city was bursting; the normal population of less than thirty thousand being extended to over one hundred thousand

Jesus, along with some of his disciples, made his way there too.

This was to be a big moment in his life. For the first time he was making a public appearance in Jerusalem that he wanted all to know about. Whether he could foresee all the developments that were to come will never be known, but of one thing he was sure: it was time to take centre stage.

There was however a difficulty. Unlike in his home territories, he was virtually unknown there by sight, and one man with a head veil is very like another. But he wanted to make himself known, he wanted to be seen, he wanted to draw the crowds.

Many had heard the stories of this man from the north, who appeared to do miracles and who preached so strongly that followers flocked to him in the hills in their thousands. Many had now heard the story of Lazarus too and wanted to see him. But how would they know him?

As ever Jesus had thought of this, and the answer was simple. He would be higher than everyone else. At this especially religious time the Jews were expected to walk into and around the Holy City, but this was not a hard and fast rule. Not for the first time Jesus ignored the rule when there was a compelling reason.

Besides, there was a precedent. There was a prophecy in the Book of Zechariah: "Tell the daughter of Zion, behold thy king cometh to thee, meek and riding upon an ass".

So Jesus sent a disciple ahead of him to find a donkey, so that when he finally entered Jerusalem he was head and shoulders above everyone else. The word quickly went round: "That's Jesus, that's the man from the north…", and even, "…that's the Messiah".

Jerusalem was already in ferment.

Both the senior Jews and the Romans knew that some of the Jews, the zealots, were near boiling point. They had had enough of the Roman rule and they had read the scriptures. They were certain that before long a new age was to dawn, a new era that would return the Jews to their rightful place of independence in their own country.

One of the zealots was a disciple: Simon (Simon the Canaanite – not to be confused with Simon Peter, usually known just as Peter). This Simon was bursting to join battle with the Romans and even the senior Jews themselves. He was desperate for Jesus to assert himself and show the warlike leadership Simon was sure he should be showing. He transmitted this zeal to the disciple Judas; together they agreed that Jesus was beginning to let them down. Neither knew what to do to hurry things up to establish the Kingdom of God on earth; they just watched and waited, looking for an opportunity to get their campaign into life.

And when Jesus was set to enter Jerusalem there were those of a historical mind who thought he was repeating the moment two centuries earlier when the reformer Simon Maccabeus had done the same and set about clearing the city of its crooked and criminal factions. Everything contributed to the feeling that something should happen *now*.

To this end a cell had been meeting; people of the Jews who were impatient to get things moving. There were half a dozen in the room, people of a fiery disposition who were determined to take the fight to the enemy and who believed the time was right.

They were fully aware that Jesus was coming and they were grasping the opportunity with both hands. Knowing that he had many followers and that hundreds, if not thousands, more would flock to see and listen to him, they were ready to take advantage of a city that needed only a little encouragement to boil over.

The fighting words flew about. "This is the time to overthrow the Roman dictators."

"The city will be full, let's move against them."

"We could get Jesus to denounce the false leaders, the accursed Romans."

"This is our opportunity."

But this posed a great problem for Jesus. Certainly he was there to preach about the new era. But to him the new era was the Kingdom of God, not civil war. He was in a hugely difficult situation, caught uncomfortably between two positions. He wanted to preach for change, but not for the change the rebellious Jews wanted.

The tension was ratcheting up. The leaders of the Jews could smell trouble in the air. The Romans could smell the same. And the verdict was identical: *Jesus must be stopped.*

But this was not easy. If they moved against him now there was every chance they would make things worse by strengthening the determination of his followers. But if they left it, it might be too late.

In the end they adopted the only measure they could: they waited.

So Jesus on his donkey entered a city high in tension to see and be seen.

He already had an inkling about what was going on. He must have known he was living dangerously, but perhaps that was exactly what he wanted. He fervently believed the Kingdom of God was at hand, and equally fervently believed it was his job and birthright to bring it to earth. Everything seemed to be happening at once; all the signs were encouraging him. In his mind there was a conjunction of birth (of the Kingdom), excitement (the city was alive as seldom before) and death (his own). There could not be a more explosive moment in the history of the Jews, nor one in which people's emotions and ambitions were more concentrated. It was the perfect scenario for the arrival of the Kingdom of God.

But before he even got in to the heart of Jerusalem something occurred which stirred up the fury of the Pharisees even further. Already expecting trouble, they watched while Jesus's followers laid down branches and twigs – and even some of their coats – in the path before him, to make his entry into Jerusalem even more triumphal.

And the followers called things out. "Praise God, for here is the Son of David". And, "Blessed is he who comes in the name of the Lord". And, "Praise God in highest heaven".

The Pharisees and High Priests of the Jews looked at one another and knew they were losing the battle. "The whole world is following him. Something must be done." But no-one knew what.

So he entered the city on his donkey, followed by his disciples and a rapidly growing crowd. And now that he was up aloft on his donkey with his contingent of followers everyone knew that this was Jesus. Within a very few minutes and less than a hundred feet inside the city walls, the crowd was engulfing him, to the immediate alarm of both the Roman soldiers and the leaders of the Jews, already seeing their worst fears on the way to becoming reality.

Yet still the Romans and the Jewish temple guard hung back, each under orders to try and keep things under control without sparking any further trouble. So the soldiers stayed in the background and the Jewish informers watched and waited.

There seemed little to worry about at first. True, Jesus was surrounded by crowds, true it would be difficult to stop them if the men started to erupt with excitement or became aggressive. But, so far at least, nothing much was happening; the crowd just followed, some calling out, some just waiting to see what developed.

In fact, nothing seemed to be developing. Jesus made no speech but just sat on his donkey in the centre of the jostling crowd and toured the city, ending up, not surprisingly, at the temple.

If the Romans and the Jewish leaders were expecting trouble here, once again it did not materialise. For Jesus simply got off the donkey and went inside, his closest disciples following behind.

And yet, all the time while nothing was happening, the pressure was building up and the city ripening for an explosion.

But it did not come for two days.

After his tour of the city and visit to the temple, Jesus simply left Jerusalem again and retired to stay the night with friends back in Bethany. The city was left wondering. The lead character in the drama that everyone was expecting had inexplicably left the stage.

But the next morning he returned and this time did not disappoint those who were looking for fireworks.

Back on his donkey he re-entered Jerusalem and made straight for the temple. As on the previous day, he was quickly surrounded and the crowd moved along with him. Unlike on his first day, he stopped several times and talked to the crowd. His voice was low, not making any attempt to excite them, but simply preaching as he had often done before, using examples from everyday life to point the way of God.

But then, something different. He looked around and saw some well-dressed people on the edge of the crowd, hiding in the shadows, watching and listening carefully. He knew these were not his followers, but people sent to spy - or even Chief Priests and Pharisees themselves. He decided to teach them a lesson.

"The story of the farmers," he called out. The crowd immediately quietened, sensing something was about to happen.

When he had their full attention, he looked over their heads for a moment, and caught the eye of the watchers. So pointed was his look that many turned round to see who he was staring at. The watchers tried to shrink away but by now they were caught in the crowd and had to stay where they were.

"A man planted a vineyard," started Jesus, "built a wall round it, installed a grape press and all that was necessary to make wine. When he had done this he let the vineyard out to tenant farmers and moved on to start work somewhere else. When it was time to pick the grapes he sent one of his servants to collect his share of the crop. But the tenant farmers wouldn't pay and beat the servant up instead. So he sent another servant to collect his share - and the farmers did the same. Finally he sent his own son, believing they would surely respect him. But it didn't work out this way. The tenant farmers said to each other, 'Here comes the son and heir. If we kill him we can keep the vineyard for ourselves.' And that is exactly what they did, murdering him and throwing his body out of the vineyard."

The crowd muttered to each other, appalled at the behaviour.

"So what do you think should happen next?" asked Jesus.

They had no answer, so he spoke quickly back to them. "I'll tell you. The original farmer will come and kill them, and then let the vineyard to others."

"Surely not," said the crowd.

"God would not approve."

"That's as barbaric as the tenant farmers."

But Jesus looked over their heads again, to the watchers in the shadows, and not for the first time spoke contentiously. "That would be the Lord's doing, and wonderful to see." Those who knew Jesus knew he was not as gentle as he was often made out to be.

Those who watched at the back found fear clutching at them. They shuffled about, realising that the point of the story was that Jesus was calling *them* the bad tenant farmers. The crowd turned and looked at them again with contempt. If there was any chance that Jesus and the Jewish leaders would see things the same way, it had gone forever.

But for the real moment of truth they had not long to wait.

He reached the temple, dismounted, and went in. A much smaller crowd followed, many reluctant to enter that holy place while they had any sort of rebellion in their hearts. The leaders of the Jews still watched and waited. The Romans did the same. All were lulled into a false sense of security. Trouble would never break out in the temple. Would it?

Jesus walked around and looked again at what he had seen the day before.

CHAPTER 3

THE FINAL STRAW

A man from the quiet north, even though used to stirring up the crowd with provocative and sometimes fiery speeches, was bound to find the lifestyle of Jerusalem extraordinarily different.

At home in Galilee, in Nazareth where Jesus had spent virtually the whole of his life, times were peaceful. It was rural, surrounded by hilly countryside, free from the pressures of business. Most of the inhabitants made their living from the land; if not farmers and shepherds, they worked at trades which supported them. There were butchers and carpenters, sheep shearers and garment stitchers, bakers and candle makers. The only real exceptions were the die factories, dotted around the lake of Galilee.

But come to bustling Jerusalem and everything is different. All the country trades are outside the city; inside are the money changers and money lenders, the businessmen and traders, the markets and the shops - bursting with customers and sellers bartering noisily over prices. Add to that the seventy thousand or so extra pilgrims arriving for the Feast of the Passover and you have a seething cauldron of a city.

Into this, on his gentle donkey, rode Jesus.

After his uneventful tour on the first day he came back on the second and made for the temple. He knew what he would see: in place of what he considered should be a quiet place of prayer and devotion, he would find a crawling mass of people engaged in commerce of all kinds.

To start with, there was the noise and the smell.

The noise came from a multitude of sources, some human, some not.

The human sounds came from merchants and money-changers. Not content with sitting and waiting for custom, the traders were shouting at the tops of their voices to attract attention. They spoke in a number of languages too; not just the local dialects, of which there were several, but also in Greek and Aramaic, in Hebrew and Latin. All were trying to outdo their neighbours. As a result it was almost impossible to hear anything.

The money-changers did excellent trade, but they had to negotiate hard to do it. Only one currency was allowed in the temple: silver drachms especially minted in the commercial centre Tyre, the only form of money considered suitable for sacred donations. And sacred donation was a huge and vital part of the temple's operation. The priests sought as much money as they could get and the people, fearful for their afterlife, responded virtuously – if unenthusiastically.

So the money-changers sat there behind their tables and accepted a variety of currencies in exchange for the silver drachms, extorting a tough rate of exchange and providing an excitable commentary on the offers and deals.

The merchants too did a brisk trade, selling all kinds of mementoes and religious artefacts. They were not so selective in their choice of currency, accepting all sizes and types of money but bartering spiritedly on every transaction. The noise was deafening.

And then there was the noise from the unhuman sources.

The temple was a place of sacrifice: thanks for a new-born babe, gratitude for a good harvest of grain, atonement for an unexplained sin, grief for a departed parent, rites of purification. All animals and birds for slaughter and sacrifice were sold within the temple walls: lambs for the rich to buy, pigeons for the poor, doves for those in between. The noise of the birds and animals waiting for slaughter and seeming to know their fate was pitiful.

And then too there was the smell. Not just from the animals themselves, which since they waited there all day and every day was considerable, but from the other end of the chain – the slaughter and burning.

There was a smell of blood, and there was a smell of roasting. Sickening to nostrils unused to it, unpleasant even to those who spent every day there.

And then there were the people walking about. The moneychangers and tradesmen couldn't work all day without refreshment and there were constant messengers and porters on the move, supplying food and drink for all the merchants.

Into this mayhem of noise and smell walked Jesus, used to the quiet synagogues of the hill country where devotion was uninterrupted by commerce. He knew he was going to do something.

At first he stood stock still. Around him were several disciples, together with a much larger crowd of onlookers who had quickly discovered who he was. And again, lurking at the back of the crowd, a little band of Pharisees, silently observing.

The sounds and the smells buffeted his head; this was a thousand miles away from what he was used to, and what he deeply believed God's house ought to be like. He did not know what to do. Slowly he moved forwards, taking in the sight and the sounds and the smells. He looked around him, and could feel a familiar sense of outrage rising within him. As with so many of the practices instigated by the Jewish leaders, he felt at odds with them.

Usually he would deal with these problems by speaking out; finding yet another way to demonstrate how the leaders were getting their priorities wrong or failing to understand the real way of God.

The disciples knew the danger signs. A look of calm would spread over his face as once again he would find a way to outwit the elders.

Back into James's mind, as he stood beside Jesus, came the event when Jesus was faced with an adulterous woman. It was one of those tests which Jesus was so good at providing. The laws of the Jews said that any women who had been found with a man who was not her husband faced only one outcome. Death by stoning. But Jesus was a forgiver. If you were genuinely sorry, he would welcome you back to his flock. Which was not the way the elders saw it.

They held the woman before him. "She must be stoned, she was with another man."

But Jesus had an answer. It was deceptively simple. "Whoever among you is without sin, he should throw the first stone."

Of course there was no answer to this. No-one was without sin except God. If you claimed to be without sin, you claimed to be God. Which was rather more of a sin than adultery.

No-one spoke. The woman was released. And for the Jewish leaders this was another nail in the coffin.

But in the temple, now, speaking out was not going to be enough. He would not even be heard.

His anger continued to rise, until he could contain it no longer. The disciples could sense danger; they always knew when he was working up to something. But they were alarmed too, for they could not see what he could achieve here – or even guess what he wanted to achieve.

He muttered: "It is written, my house shall be the house of prayer". He said it quietly to himself and only one or two of the disciples heard it. They were frightened, because beneath those mild words they could hear the undercurrent of fury.

He walked a few steps further; up to one of the moneychangers' tables, and spoke directly to the trader, "It is written," he said again, "my house shall be the house of prayer…for all nations…". He stared at the moneylender, willing him to understand. But the moneychanger was too busy with his trade, continuing to call out the rates of exchange to attract business.

Jesus stood right before him, his two hands on the front of the table. Still the trader took no notice, still the disciples stood back, fearful of what was to come. And even now they had not guessed.

Jesus spoke again, "… but you have made it a den of thieves".

Then he silently raised the front of the table with his hands and tipped it forwards towards the trader. All the baskets of coins toppled over and showered the moneychanger, who had fallen back in amazement. The time of quietness was over for Jesus. "You have made it a den of thieves" he roared and threw the table forwards towards the moneychanger.

"And you. And you. And you." Table after table he threw over, the coins hurtling to the floor, the moneychangers reeling back in amazement.

Still caught up in his own fury, Jesus started pushing some of the other traders towards the gates of the temple. In their surprise they hardly resisted but allowed themselves to be shepherded away.

Then Jesus turned his attention to the animal and bird sellers, setting free the birds, cutting the lambs loose, overturning the tables, pushing the traders away from their positions, tipping up the water skins and pitchers that the servants were carrying to and fro.

Pandemonium set in. Hardly quiet before, the temple was now in uproar, with the traders beginning to rally and come back to their places. The disciples cowered away, not for the first time alarmed at the strength of Jesus's reaction and worried at the retribution that was bound to come.

But Jesus was not caring. Moving swiftly around and with such a look of fury and outrage in his face, few felt encouraged to challenge him.

"Come," he called to his small band of disciples, "we will leave this den of thieves."

Together they left the temple and went back to Bethany.

But the repercussions were already beginning. The Pharisees, ever watchful, had seen and noted everything. They passed the news on to the Chief Priests and Scribes, who talked among themselves. And the view was always the same: he must be stopped. If stopping meant death, so be it. As Caiaphas had already said, perhaps the death of one man was the best way in any case.

So far they had discussed the situation in a rather academic sort of way. But now they were getting frightened; they had seen at first hand the power of Jesus in front of the crowd. And even though some of them were alarmed at the strength of his attitudes, many were simply delighted and revelling in the leadership this man from the hills was providing and the uncaring way in which he dared to confront the rulings of the leading Jews.

Here at last was a man with such self-belief that nothing and no-one was going to stop him. Here was the real leader. He must be the Messiah.

Faced with this the Scribes and Chief Priests knew that the time had come to start planning for Jesus's removal. For they could see how the people were turning to follow him. The more who followed him, the more the Chief Priests were losing their position. And always, at the back of their minds, was the attitude of the Romans. If they saw this new army rising up and taking strength from this powerful new leader, it wouldn't be long before they too brought reprisals on the whole of the Jews. The Chief Priests had a lot to lose and they saw it as their duty to fight back and reclaim their position.

He may have retired to Bethany after the outburst but he had no fear about returning.

The next morning, still accompanied by his disciples, who continued to be alarmed at the goings-on, he went back into the temple.

The babble had returned as noisily as ever. The traders were shouting, the animals were crying, the servants were marching, the smells just as strong. Lost in the crowd, he was unnoticed by the stallholders.

But not by the Chief Priests and elders of the temple, who were waiting to challenge him.

A small party of them stopped in front of him.

"You are Jesus of Nazareth?" It was more a statement than a question. "He who overthrew the moneychangers' tables? And speaks against the leaders of the Jews?"

Jesus made no reply but just stood still and looked at them.

"Answer us this," they said, laying a trap. "By whose authority do you behave this way? Who gave you this right?"

They had chosen the wrong person to try and trap with words. No-one was better at turning the tables on his interrogators.

"All right," he said. "I will ask one thing of you. Answer that and I will answer you."

It seemed reasonable. They nodded.

"The baptism of John," said Jesus, referring to his cousin John the Baptist, whom most of the Jewish elders had refused to recognise despite his popularity among the people. "Was that done at a sign from heaven, or carried out by man?"

The elders had set a trap, but they were the ones caught up in one. Whichever way they answered would be wrong.

If they said, "from heaven", Jesus would answer, "So why did you not believe in him?".

If they said, "by man", they would find themselves up against the multitudes who followed him and believed him a true prophet.

They could find no answer to the question. "We cannot tell," they said at last.

"So neither do I tell you by what authority I do my work."

He had won the battle, but the war went on.

He walked away, followed half-heartedly by the elders, who felt they had been outmanoeuvred but were not ready to give up yet. He crossed the temple court and came to the treasury, the area with the huge pots into which people cast their donations towards the upkeep of the temple.

He and the disciples stood watching while rich people came and threw huge sums of money into the caskets. He saw how the Scribes and elders smiled and nodded approvingly as these Jews paved the way for their future in heaven.

And then a different sort of donor. A tiny elderly widow, dressed in traditional costume, approached, dug into the folds of her garments, produced two mites – the smallest denomination there was – and gently slipped them over the rim of a casket.

Jesus saw the reaction among the Jewish elders; contempt for the size of the donation in comparison with what had gone before.

Glancing towards the elders and the Scribes, he called his disciples closer and said loudly to them so that the elders could hear, "This poor widow has put in more than all those who threw so much. For they were only sparing a little of what they had got, but this poor woman has given everything she has".

He looked challengingly at the elders. They recalled those comments of his that had been relayed to them earlier, that they loved to go in great clothes and be recognised in the marketplaces, to sit in the best rooms at feasts. Just a few of them felt a little sheepish. But only a few. Others set him another trap.

It was not yet open warfare between the elder Jews and the Romans on the one hand and Jesus on the other. But it was warfare nevertheless.

His opposers hatched a plan. They despatched one Pharisee and one Roman to go up to him and in a friendly way ask a question. It seemed innocent enough.

Ingratiatingly the Pharisee called him Master and said, "We know you're a totally honest man and let no-one influence you in what you really believe. We understand the way you see things; you put God before man, as we all do. And you follow God's laws rather than man's. We appreciate that and understand it and know exactly what you mean. But it raises a problem when it comes to Caesar's authority as opposed to God's. And we'd like to understand how to deal with it."

The Roman stood silent, arms folded, wondering how Jesus was going to extract himself from this. The Roman needed to say nothing; just watch how the Jew would incriminate himself.

The Pharisee added, "So who is the more important, God or the leaders of the Jews as they uphold the faith? Or the Romans who rule us?"

It sounded so reasonable. How could Jesus square regarding God as the only leader, but at the same time acknowledge the authority of the Romans or the elders?

It was a neat trap. To say that the leaders mattered more than God was a betrayal of all he was supposed to believe. Say the leaders mattered less was to deny the leadership of the Jews and the leadership of the nation. And that was simultaneously denial of the Jewish faith and treason.

But as ever Jesus saw through the hypocrisy.

"Are you tempting me?"

"Of course not, we just want to know whether you think it is lawful, say, to give tribute to Caesar."

"Bring me a penny."

Someone handed him a penny.

"Whose is this image on it? Whose name is inscribed over it?"

"Caesar's, of course."

"There is your answer. Give to Caesar what is Caesar's, and to God what is God's."

In his answer Jesus had actually said many things.

Firstly he had stifled the question; the answer was obvious in a way but the way he had framed it left his inquisitors nowhere to go in the argument and they fell silent for want of anything else to say.

But for those who looked below the surface of his reply there was something far more fundamental.

Jesus did not want a war with the Romans. There could be only one outcome from that: the destruction of the Jews. The way to win the hearts and minds of the Jews and to make certain the coming of the Kingdom of God was to persuade them of his own views, however they may vary from the traditional teaching of the senior Jews.

So far as he was concerned the leadership-on-earth question was completely irrelevant. He just had to make the others see it. It didn't matter to him one jot what everyone thought about Caesar or the views of the Pharisees or however importantly they regarded them. The only thing that mattered was the coming of the Kingdom of God. So if he could encourage them to give Caesar suitable deference as an earthly leader that would avoid trouble and leave his own race free to get on with what really mattered.

It was a fine idea. Unfortunately it was above them. They only saw and heard what they wanted to see and hear. They – both the leaders of the Jews and the Romans – had already come to the conclusion that he had to be stopped before he created chaos and carnage.

Once again he had deflected open criticism by his deft "Give to Caesar what is Caesar's" answer. But they could see how he had walked round them again and it only made them the more determined to finish him once and for all.

Before long however there was another confrontation; further ammunition in their war against him.

After this exchange Jesus and his small band left the temple.

Once outside, one of the disciples said, "Just look at this temple. Isn't it an amazing thing? The sheer size, the *grandness* of it."

The disciple expected Jesus to agree. Whatever he thought of the way it had come to be used, he couldn't deny its magnificence. But, as ever, his reply was not at all what was expected.

Instead of agreeing, or even discussing it, he said, "Yes – but you see these great buildings? I tell you, there will not be one stone standing on top of another; it will all be thrown down."

The disciples were speechless, not beginning to understand what he meant.

"But it had taken forty-six years to build."

"It will all go."

He was prophesying. And then he went on to talk in a way that as so often they didn't understand. "But I also say, destroy this temple and in three days I will restore it."

They took him literally. And repeated, "It took forty-six years to build and you will build it up again in three days?"

Despite his sorrow at their not understanding him, he smiled. As usual, he was asking too much of them. As usual he was teaching by example. He was not talking about the temple before them, but the temple of the body. He was talking about resurrection and everlasting life.

But some of the Pharisees had heard his words and took them back to the elders.

"He is saying he could rebuild the temple in three days if it were destroyed. What man could do that? It is blasphemy. Again."

It was the final straw. Now the plotting for his death began in earnest.

CHAPTER 4

THE LAST SUPPER

But Jesus was not sitting about and waiting for death. He might have known it was coming but he had a lot to do before then. Not least because the Passover itself was almost upon them and he had to prepare for it. As the last free act of his life it was almost impossible to overstate its importance; what would happen that night would echo through the rest of history.

He called one of the lesser known disciples, James the son of Alphaeus, to him and said, "It is the Passover tomorrow. I want you and all the other disciples to join me for the meal, but we must find somewhere suitable. We do not know Jerusalem well; can you go and find such a place? It is *the* most important meal; find a good place, a place with room for us all where we can be in comfort and in peace. Tell whoever you find that your master says his time has come and that he wants to keep the Passover in your house with his disciples."

James set off. As Jesus said, they did not know Jerusalem well and he had no idea where to start. He walked through the town, automatically making his way towards the temple. He passed one or two inns, but felt that such a place of commerce – a little like the temple itself, it seemed – would not be suitable. He started asking people but it was not until he arrived at the temple walls that he had success. A man knew someone who had a house with a large upstairs room he sometimes let out for dinners and parties and meetings.

He found his way there and was shown the room. It seemed to fulfil everything that Jesus had asked for: a good size, and a good table, set across one end of a long room.

"There will be twelve of us," said James, "and I expect a couple of us will want to come ahead to prepare the table and the room. I'm not sure who it'll be. Can we make some sort of arrangement to meet? There are too many streets all looking the same; they'll never find it if I try and describe it."

"I'll send one of my servants," said the owner. "He'll be at the

Ginnoth Gate. I'll get him to carry a pitcher of water so they know him."

"Carry a pitcher? That's woman's work."

"Exactly. So he will stand out and you'll quickly recognise him."

James thanked and left him, returning to Jesus pleased he had been able to carry out his master's request. He couldn't have known that he had found the location for one of the most famous meals of all time.

The elders and the Scribes and the Chief Priests were having yet another consultation. They were at the palace of the High Priest, Ciaphas.

"It must be now, before he does any more damage," said a Scribe.

"Yes," said another eagerly, "let's get it over and done with. He must be put to death *now*."

"But – " said a third, "is this the right time? On a feast day?"

They argued among themselves, trying to find a way to carry out the sentence without causing a riot when he had so many followers and on such a holy day. But in the end caution won. Grudgingly they all finally agreed that to take Jesus on the day of Passover was inviting trouble, though it would have to be soon.

The meeting was about to break up when a servant entered and whispered to Ciaiphas. Caiaphas looked surprised and conversed quietly with the servant, then turned to the room and said, "We have an unexpected visitor. I am told we should see him and hear what he has to say".

But before the servant could usher the visitor in, one of the elders stood up.

"I know who this is and I know why he is here. It is someone I have been talking to in the interests of settling this whole matter. I have asked him to come tonight because I think – we all think – the time is near to resolve the problem and this man will help us do it."

Ciaiphas looked surprised. "You know the man?"

"I have met him once or twice. He is one of Jesus's followers. His name is Judas Iscariot, a man of Kerioth, a village outside Galilee. He is the only one of the disciples not to come from Jesus's home land; he does not have quite the same affiliation as the others."

"So why is he here?"

"Let him come in and I'll explain."

Ciaiphas nodded to the servant who opened the door and ushered Judas in.

"This is Judas," the elder continued. "He will help us in our task. If we take Jesus we must do so at night, so we do not attract attention. And it is hard to tell one man from another in the dark, especially when his head is covered by the veil. When the time comes – and I think it must be very soon – we are going to need someone to identify him to our soldiers. Judas will do this for us; he has agreed. For a certain sum of money, of course."

Ciaiphas felt he should regain control of the meeting. As it happened he had heard of Judas; his information network worked well. "And why would you do this?" he asked of Judas. "Are you not one of this man's most trusted friends? I have heard it said you are one of those Jesus loves the most."

Judas looked back at the elder who had introduced him. A questioning look, that said, "Must I respond to that?"

The elder nodded. "We have to trust one another," he said. "You have to give your reasons or we are bound to wonder what is really in your mind. Perhaps it is just the money, although it must be said thirty pieces of silver is not so very much."

Judas was in a dilemma. He had a reason for betraying Jesus, but he could not give it. Like all Jews he believed that salvation would only come to Israel through suffering and death: just as the Passover lamb was slaughtered as a ritual sacrifice. Judas's view was that Jesus should *become* the Passover lamb. He believed in everything that Jesus was saying and doing. But he was not doing it fast enough. In Judas's mind the sacrifice of Jesus would hasten the coming of the Kingdom of God. In his mind Jesus had not fulfilled his promise; things were beginning to go wrong. Somehow Jesus had become associated with a quite separate rebellion against the Romans and this was becoming a diversion. By sacrificing Jesus he *must* be helping to bring about the re-establishment of Jewish supremacy. But he could hardly explain all this to those he knew were enemies of what Jesus stood for.

Instead he said the only thing he could. "It is for the money."

They accepted it; what else could they do?

"What will you do?" asked one of the elders.

"You are going to take him at night?" said Judas, already guessing the answer from his previous conversations with the elder. "I will help your men identify him. When I know where he will be after the Passover meal I will come and tell you. I shall be there too and will identify him with an embrace. Then they will be sure who they are arresting."

Ciaiphas and the elders and Scribes exchanged glances. This was quicker than they had anticipated. But it was an opportunity that seemed to be foolproof – and it had been handed to them. The arrest would be at night, when other Jews were probably still at their Passover meal and the Romans out of the way. And they now had a guarantee of arresting the right person. It was an opportunity they could not refuse.

There were two disciples named James. One – James the son of Alphaeus – was the one who had already been into Jerusalem to arrange the place for the Passover meal. Now Jesus called the other James – one of the two sons of Zebadee – and Simon Peter the fisherman to him.

"I want you to go into the city and prepare the place for our Passover meal. Just inside the Ginnoth Gate you will find a man bearing a pitcher of water. He will lead you to the house as James has arranged. Just say to the man of the house the Master asks where the guest chamber is where we shall eat our meal. He will show you a large room upstairs. Go and make ready for us."

James and Simon Peter did as he said, prepared the room, and returned to Bethany.

When it was time to leave for the Passover meal in the evening, Jesus called all twelve disciples to him and they set off together in a band. As they walked towards the city, Jesus was in the centre of them. The atmosphere seemed to be cheerful. The disciples were looking forward to the Passover meal and to being together with their master. None of them had any premonition of trouble.

Except – there was a slight sense of unease at the back of some of their minds. Perhaps it was a left-over emotion from the scene at the temple, a little feeling that they would be remembered for being a part of it. Perhaps walking into the city as a group made them feel more visible and exposed. Perhaps the sense that they could never be quite sure what Jesus would do next was beginning to get to them.

Slowly this feeling began to overcome them and one by one they fell silent. And then Jesus spoke to them with words they couldn't believe and didn't wish to understand.

"I am going to tell you things that will happen in Jerusalem, so that you are strong and prepared."

The words did nothing to calm them but served only to heighten the sense of unease and fear that was beginning to overtake them. Silently they looked at each other, then at their master, taking the lead as they walked.

He went on with words that terrified them; the more so for the quiet way in which he delivered them.

"The Son of Man is going to be betrayed and delivered to those who oppose him - the Chief Priests and the Scribes. They will condemn him to death and turn him over to the Romans. He will be mocked and tortured and spat upon. He will be killed."

The prophecy was at first received with silence, then with a mutter of disbelief and rejection. But their words petered out; they could find nothing to say.

Judas was especially shocked. He could not decide whether Jesus knew what he had been planning, or this was some extraordinary coincidence.

Jesus looked at them and then offered a final sentence. It was designed to encourage them but they were so shocked by what they had already heard that it fell into the continuing silence.

"But on the third day he shall rise again."

The disciples looked between themselves with faces that were struggling to come to terms with what Jesus had said. They had come to realise they were living dangerously, unable to predict what Jesus might say or do next. They knew they had enemies in Jerusalem - as they seemed to be having everywhere they went - and now their worst fears were being realised as Jesus foretold the outcome of his teaching.

Silently they continued on their way to the city, each struggling with his own thoughts, each trying not to let his face show the anguish he was suffering. Jesus alone marched steadfastly along, knowing his fate and knowing it was his father's almighty plan for him and the Jews.

All twelve disciples were gathered in the upper room.

Simon Peter, usually called just Peter, and his brother Andrew, both fishermen. James and John, sons of Zebadee, also fishermen. Mathew, a tax collector. James, son of Alphaeus. Thaddeus, also known as Judas son of James – and as Lebbaeus too. Simon the zealot from Canaan. Philip. Bartholomew. Thomas. And Judas Iscariot.

The room was big, with a grand table extending right across it at one end. As the disciples looked around and began to settle themselves, Jesus surprised them. As he had so often.

He took off his outer clothes and wrapped a towel around himself. He looked across to Thomas and gestured towards a large bowl of water. "Bring it here."

Thomas brought the bowl and Jesus called Bartholomew to him.

"Bartholomew, come to me and stand before me." With no idea what was going on, Bartholomew did as his master requested.

And then, to everyone's astonishment, Jesus proceeded to wash the disciple's feet, and then to dry them with the towel he had wrapped around himself. Bewildered, Bartholomew stood back and Jesus called Thaddeus across and did the same. The disciples looked at each other but dared not ask the question until at last Jesus called Peter.

Peter, braver than the others, asked the question that was on everyone's mind.

"Master – why do you wash my feet?"

The answer was not clear. "You will not understand what I am doing now. But it will become clear later."

Peter was not ready to accept this. "Lord, you will never wash my feet. It is not right that you should do this."

But Jesus replied, "If I do not wash you, you shall have no part in things with me."

This was too much for Peter who, as ever, could quickly be

persuaded by Jesus's words. He swung the other way. "In that case, wash not just my feet but also my hands and my head."

"It is not necessary. A person who is bathed does not need to be washed all over – only the feet which tread the dust." And then he looked around the room, and went on: "So I say to you, you *are* clean. Except one of you."

This was the first hint there was a traitor in the midst. But no-one, other than Judas, could understand what he meant. And, used as they were not always to grasp what he was getting at, they kept their puzzlement to themselves.

But he had not quite finished. "Do you know what I have done to you? You call me Master, and that is right, for that is what I am to you. The servant is not as important as the master, and neither is the messenger as important as he who sends him. So if I wash your feet, I have set an example which you should follow; you do not need to question me, neither should you. Just do the same as I have done and wash each other's feet. I have explained this to you; do as I say and you will be happy."

Now the disciples sat down for the Passover meal. Or rather, they *reclined,* symbolic of their freedom from bondage – unlike slaves who had had to eat their meals standing.

Noticeably absent was any female company. Not his mother, not his friend Mary Magdalene, not Lazarus's sisters Mary and Martha, not any of his other female followers. Perhaps he knew the meal would end in tragedy and wanted to spare them the sadness. Perhaps he expected harsh words from those disciples he knew were beginning to feel a little disappointed in him.

He knew he was about to be betrayed; equally he knew not everyone would understand what was happening, so perhaps he just wanted to be with those he had chosen to follow him.

So as they reclined in their low chairs, he looked about him, his mind overflowing with conflicting emotions. He was with friends; he was with one who would betray him and another who would deny him; he was on the verge of that fateful step which should lead to the coming of the Kingdom of God on earth. It was his greatest moment and his worst.

The Passover meal, known later as the *seder*, commemorated the Jewish peoples' release from Egyptian bondage fifteen hundred years earlier. As commanded by God to Moses and the Hebrews of the time, a lamb was prepared and roasted, ready to be eaten with bitter herbs and matzos - unleavened bread, cooked in this way in memory of the little time the Jews had to prepare to flee their Egyptian slavery, kneaded and baked in just eighteen minutes.

The meal started. But it was not the usual celebration the disciples were looking for. One after another, events unfolded which confused, surprised and shocked them all.

It started with a dire warning; a remark from Jesus which put them all on edge.

Just as they had poured the wine and taken their first sips, Jesus said quietly without warning, "One of you is going to betray me".

Shocked, they stopped in their tracks, glasses on the way to their mouths, hands on the way to the dishes in the centre of the table. They looked first at Jesus, and then at each other, suspicion on every face. "Is it me?" they asked, then in their faces the question as they looked around at each other, "Is it you?"

Jesus replied to only one of the disciples, his answer drowned by the questions and appalled remarks of the others. To Judas, who had asked the same question, Jesus replied quietly, "You are saying it". Judas said nothing more, avoiding Jesus's eyes and wondering how on earth Jesus could have known. He had no idea what to do and bent his head to his meal, aware that his master's eyes were still on him.

The other disciples continued to ask, "Is it me?"

Jesus answered at last, but said nothing to put their minds at rest. Rather he worried them still further. "It is he who dips his hand with me in the dish." Then he dipped a morsel of bread into the soup before them and handed it to Judas.

But since they had all begun to dip their hands in the dishes to help themselves to food the gesture passed unnoticed. His words had done nothing to calm them; it had only underlined Jesus's statement that it would be one of the twelve present who would betray him.

"The scriptures have foretold it and I shall go as it is written. But I say, it would be better for that man if he had not been born." It was his only admission of bitterness about what was to befall him.

The sounds of the disciples' questions fell away for a moment as they absorbed what their master had said, then suddenly Babel was let loose and they all spoke at once, turning to each other, shocked and appalled at the thought that Jesus was to be betrayed – and by one of those at the table. Each looked around, wondering whether his neighbour, or the one at the end of the table, or the one now looking at him, was the betrayer. Suddenly they all felt lost. Instead of being part of a tight-knit band following a great leader, they had a traitor in the midst. Their world was starting to fall apart.

Gradually the sounds of their worried voices faded away. Unable to decide what else to do, hesitantly they started on their meal again.

Before long, Jesus spoke again, as if nothing had happened.

He took some bread, broke it and blessed it, and said, "Take some, eat it, think of this as my body." He distributed it around the table.

And then he did the same with the wine, giving thanks and saying, "Drink all of this. Think of this as my blood, my testament to a new future, which will be shed to forgive you your sins."

The words froze them again. The reference to his blood being shed for them frightened them. Coming so soon after being told one of them was to betray him, it reinforced the dread.

Again they looked at each other, desperately hoping they were misunderstanding and that their leader would say something to explain and relieve their worries. But his next words made it clear that they were on the very verge of the biggest moment of their lives.

"This is the last wine I shall drink until we drink all together in my father's kingdom."

Again, silence settled upon the table. The tension in the room could be felt by everyone; that icy feeling that invades the body when you know something of the greatest significance has happened, when you know that life will never be the same again.

Jesus was apparently not going to say anything further, at least for the time being, and once again the disciples half-heartedly reached for their food and their wine in an attempt to bring some sort of normality to the meal.

According to tradition they ate roast lamb. And also according to tradition they embarked on four glasses of red wine each. Every Jewish person at the time of Passover was expected to drink these four glasses – even the poorest For this to be able to happen alms were collected.

Jesus leaned across and said to Judas, not making any attempt to keep his voice down, "Hurry – do it now".

Judas was keeper of the disciples' purse and no-one was surprised when he left the room. They assumed he was going out to pay for the meal they had just consumed. Or to give alms to cover the four glasses each of them had drank. He was just going about his normal business as their treasurer.

Except that Jesus knew he wasn't.

CHAPTER 5

ARREST

As Judas left, Jesus knew this was the start of the final act of his life.

But to the disciples he was positive; this was the beginning of the beginning, not the beginning of the end. He said, "We are entering the moment of glory. Of my glory, and God's glory in me."

The disciples looked from one to another. He had already frightened them by saying he was about to die. What exactly was he meaning now he was talking of glory? But if they were confused by that, they were even more confused by what he was to say next. Often puzzling them, his next words made no sense at all.

"We have very little time together left. Where I am going, you cannot come. I said this to the leaders of the Jews and I say it to you too."

Peter spoke up for all of them and asked the question on everyone's mind: "Lord – *where* are you going?"

"Where I am going you cannot follow me – now. But you will be able to later."

Peter spoke again. "Why can't I follow you now? If need be I would lay down my life for you."

Jesus looked back at him steadily. The room was silent; everyone was listening. "Will you really lay down your life for my sake? In truth I do not think you will. In fact by the time the cock has crowed you will deny three times that you even know me. In fact you will all deny me. Remember what the scriptures say? 'God will strike the shepherd, and the sheep of the flock will be scattered'. You will all desert me at first, just as the sheep."

Peter spoke again. "Even if everyone else deserts you, I will not, even if I have to go to prison for you."

Jesus repeated, "You will all desert me – at first. But listen to what I say: I have a new commandment for you. Love each other, just as I have loved you. If you do this in public everyone will know that you are my disciples. Use this love and turn to each other and give strength to each other. And then one day, when this is over, you will be able to recognise what you have done and be sorry for denying me."

There was confusion in the room. Peter - to deny three times that he knew Jesus? All of them - to desert him? And Jesus himself? Going away where they could not follow him now but would be able to later?

They waited in silence for whatever Jesus might say next. They felt a little reassured by his next remarks.

"Don't let your heart be troubled. I am going to my father, where there is room for everyone. I will prepare places for you, and then I will come and find you so that in the end we shall all be together. You *know* where I am going."

But the disciple Thomas, who would doubt Jesus later, also doubted now. "Lord, we do not know where you are going. How can we know the way?"

Jesus replied, "I *am* the way, the truth, the light. If you know me, you know my father too".

Philip was not too sure either. "Show us the father and we shall believe."

Jesus was beginning to be a little tired of this. He took a deep breath. "Have I been with you all this time and still you don't know, Philip? I have told you, if you have seen me, you have seen the father. So whyever are you saying show us the father? Do you not believe that I and the father are one? Listen: I am in the father, and the father is in me. You can ask for anything in my name and I will do it, for whatever I do will bring glory to the father. If you love me, do what I ask."

When Judas left the room, as Jesus knew, he didn't go to pay for the food they had eaten, neither did he give money so that the poorer Jews could afford to drink their customary four glasses of wine. He made his way to the house of one of the Chief Priests.

"Have you come with news?" asked the priest.

Judas was already beginning to feel uncomfortable. He knew why he was doing this, but it went against much that he believed in. Certainly he didn't think Jesus was making things happen fast enough; certainly he had hoped and expected that Jesus would form a fighting army to re-establish the independence of the Jews in their own country. He was disappointed that none of this was happening and was now persuading himself that the way ahead lay in another direction. Now he believed that by bringing about Jesus's death he would be forcing the issue. The Kingdom of God must come more quickly to rescue Jesus himself.

But… He was still betraying his master. He was still betraying the Son of God, if Jesus himself was to be believed. He felt hopelessly torn. Whatever he did was wrong, yet he firmly believed it was also right.

"Yes, I have news. I know where my master will go later tonight, where he – and we – often go. It'll be evening time so most people will be in their homes, and it will be dark too. He is going to a garden in Gethsamene."

The priest didn't know it.

"Across the Kidron valley at the foot of the Mount of Olives. He and his followers will be there later. It is called Gethsemane: "valley of oil". You will see him and his disciples in the garden there."

The priest didn't care about the names of places. He did care very much about catching Jesus, and he was not going to leave any stones unturned.

"How shall we know him? You'll all look the same in the dark with your veils. We need a sign. The last thing we want to do is arrest the wrong person."

"I have already said, I will give you a sign," said Judas, impatient that the arrangements were apparently not tied down. "Get your men there and when I arrive I will go over to Jesus and welcome him with an embrace. They can ask him too; he will never deny himself. There will be no difficulty."

"God go with you," said the Chief Priest. "You will receive your reward, as arranged. And you will receive your reward in heaven too. You are doing a great service to the Jews; we cannot allow this man to cause the sort of trouble I see coming. He must be stopped and we thank you."

The words should have comforted Judas.

But they didn't. He felt that logic and good common sense were on his side. But deep down he was already hating himself.

No-one had thought very much about Judas's departure. There

were always things to do, and Judas, as the keeper of the disciples' purse, was often going about a little business.

The meal continued – as it did with everyone celebrating the Passover throughout Jerusalem – precisely in accordance with Old Testament commandments. The sacrificial lamb could be either sheep or goat; it should be less than one year old and unblemished. After it was killed in the evening but before it was roasted, its blood should be smeared on each side of the door and over the top, as God's sign that this house should be spared.

The lamb was roasted and garnished with bitter herbs. The disciples drank their customary four glasses of wine. And they tried to talk.

But it was not easy. They had been unnerved by Jesus's forecasting of his own death and all were aware of the drama that was beginning to be played out. Perhaps, subconsciously, they all were beginning to realise that Jesus himself was becoming a symbolic sacrifice. The Old Testament books had foretold it often enough.

At the end of the meal and before they set off for Gethsemane, they sang a hymn, the Hallel, reminding them of the deliverance of the Jews from the Egyptians. Taken from the Book of Psalms, the phrases both spelled out the joy of their beliefs and dark hints of what was to come.

"I love the Lord, because he has heard my voice and my supplication… I found trouble and sorrow… then I called upon the name of the Lord in distress and the Lord answered me and set me in a great place… I shall not die but live and declare the works of the Lord…"

Together they all walked to the garden of Gethsemane: an orchard with trees bearing apples and pears, small oranges and figs, in a "valley of oil". Yet despite being a place where nature was at its most bountiful, where the fruit was hanging heavily upon the branches, there was an air of sadness about the place. Even at night, as it now was, with the few candles and lanterns the disciples had brought, there was a sense of melancholy, as though a stage had been set ready for a tragedy.

When they arrived, Jesus called three of them to his side: James, John and Simon Peter the fisherman. "Come with me a little further;

stay and keep watch while I pray."

They walked on a little in the darkness and then Jesus stopped. Peter held a lantern to Jesus's face and was distraught at what he found.

"Master…?" he faltered, unable to find words to express the sadness he saw.

Jesus looked back at him, his mind overflowing. Slowly he said, "Yes, my soul is suffering. The sadness I feel is overwhelming, a sadness even to death. Wait. Stay here and watch while I pray. And you too, pray. Pray that you do not fall into temptation".

The disciples, shocked and overawed at what was happening, were only too glad to be given the opportunity to stay behind. Each of them was already finding it too hard to bear. As Jesus went on without them they sank to the ground, each feeling a mixture of exhaustion and fear.

And that mixture had the effect it always has: the mind and body slows down and comes to the rescue by shutting away the emotions. Despite Jesus's warning about not falling into temptation, the disciples gave in. They fell asleep.

A hundred feet away, Jesus cast himself on the ground and prayed. He prayed as never before, concentrating and compelling his mind into absolute communion with his father. The concentration was so acute that it induced a great pressure against his blood vessels and caused some to burst. So intense that perspiration poured from him; perspiration that was tinted by the redness of blood.

He knew he was on the verge of the greatest - and the hardest - moment of his life. He wondered if he could bear it, if he was strong enough to accept such demands. The human side of him took over and unable to stop his own words, he prayed, "Oh my father, if it is possible, take this responsibility from me, it is more than I can manage." And then, remembering who he was and what he had to do, he added, "Nevertheless, it is not what I want, but your will that must be fulfilled".

He returned to the three disciples and found them asleep, despite his warning to them.

He shook his head in disappointment and then gently nudged Peter awake. "Peter - you are asleep? Could you not keep watch for me for one hour? Your spirit might be willing, but your flesh is weak." James and John awoke too and he repeated to them all, "Watch and pray that you do not again enter into temptation".

He went away to pray some more.

And returned to find them asleep once again.

He spoke quietly to them, repeating what he had said. They looked back at him in embarrassment, unable to find any words to excuse themselves.

Again he went forward to pray. And again when he returned they had found their eyelids too heavy and were once again asleep on the ground.

This time, knowing their human weakness and the fear they were suffering, he said only, "Sleep on now, take your rest." He looked down at them, his eyes moist with understanding. To himself he said, "There will time enough for you to be awake. The time is almost here. The Son of Man is about to be betrayed into the hands of sinners."

And then, later, louder to wake them up, "Come, rise up, we must go. He who is to betray me is near."

They were quickly wide awake. And they were terrified.

Together they made their way back to the other disciples. Like the three Jesus had taken with him, many of them too had lain on the ground and fallen asleep. Others had prayed, though they were not quite sure what for. Others had just stood around, trying to find things to say but unable to make sense of their situation.

As Jesus and his little band returned they could hear sounds from the distance. And through the trees of the orchard, flickering lights were beginning to make themselves seen. The lights of lanterns and burning torches, making their way towards them.

The disciples fell silent, watching and then listening. For as the lights became close, so could the sounds begin to be heard. The sounds of many men walking, of the slight clanking of the dress of soldiers, the regular step as what seemed to be a small army approached.

Through the trees they came, breaking from the cover and then stopping facing Jesus and his disciples. They wore the uniform of law enforcers; Jewish police who reported only to the Chief Priests and Pharisees, and a few Roman soldiers, keeping a watchful eye to report back to their leaders.

Jesus looked steadily back at them as they stood there with their lights, their staves and swords. There were many of them, far more than was necessary to arrest just one man – especially one who would make no attempt to defend himself.

And then from behind them stepped one more man, a man not in uniform.

It was Judas.

Almost unnoticed in the patchy darkness and unheard among the sounds of the soldiers, Judas slipped quietly up to Jesus and embraced him. "Hail Master," he said, and kissed him on the cheek.

Quietly, so the other disciples did not hear, Jesus replied, "My friend, why are you doing this? Do you betray the Son of Man with a kiss?"

Judas could not answer and melted away in the darkness. But he had done what he had promised; he had identified his Master in public.

The leader of the soldiers stepped forward.

Jesus, knowing what was happening, stepped forward too and asked quietly, "Who do you seek?"

"Jesus of Nazareth," said the leader.

"That is me."

Jesus anticipated being arrested there and then. But just for a moment things did not go as expected. The very sounds of the words, "Jesus… that is me", had a strange effect. The Jewish soldiers all knew the stories about Jesus, even if they hadn't known him by sight. Many of them had sometimes believed like the disciples that one day he would come to lead the Jews into war and help overthrow the hated Romans. Realising that their task now was to arrest the man in whom they had had such hopes stopped them in their tracks. It was one thing to be told to arrest someone; it was quite another to see him in person and remember just who he was.

Instead of stepping forward to arrest him they stepped back, as though they could not bring themselves to do the deed.

So Jesus asked again, "Who do you seek?"

"Jesus of Nazareth."

Jesus said, "I have told you that is me. And if it is me who you want, let my people go away; they are guilty of nothing." As he said it he was aware of the prophecy he was fulfilling: 'I have caused none of those you gave me to be lost'.

The soldiers started to do as they were commanded and stepped forward to take Jesus. But then a small scuffle broke out. Several of the disciples tried to prevent Jesus from being arrested. Peter grabbed a sword from one of the soldiers, flashed it through the air and caught the right ear of one of the high priests' servants, a man called Malchus, slicing it right off.

But before he could do anything further, Jesus restrained him.

"Put the sword down. For anyone who lives by the sword will also die by it." He went over to Malchus and touched him. "You will not suffer further," he said. And as so often in the past, the words of Jesus and the power that shone from his eyes overcame the pain the man was feeling.

Jesus returned to Peter and spoke to him again. "Do you not think I could pray to my father and he would immediately give me twelve legions of angels to protect me? But if I were to do that, how would the scriptures be fulfilled? What must be must be. Should I not drink the cup that my father has given me? Should I not accept his will? Allow this to happen."

Once again Jesus faced the soldiers. He had one last thing to say.

"Why do you come out, as though I were a thief, to take me with swords and staves? I was with the people in the temple and you did not take me then. You stretched no hands out to grasp me. But I know that this is the hour. And this is the darkness that must be."

They had had enough. Subduing their doubts, the soldiers came forward, bound him and prepared to lead him away.

The disciples stood, uncertain. Then fear overcame nearly all of them and they deserted him, hurrying off into the darkness, just as Jesus had said they would.

Only three remained.

One made a final attempt to protect his master and pull him back from the soldiers, but they grabbed hold of his robe as he struggled and tore it from him. Naked, he too fled.

As the soldiers led Jesus away, only two men were left. Peter and Philip, who followed silently in the shadows.

CHAPTER 6

THE FIRST TRIAL: ANNAS

Peter and Philip did not speak to each other. Each was too concerned with his own thoughts and frightened at the way things were developing. Each knew they were present at a momentous time: everything they had known and believed and understood over the years since they had started following Jesus was about to crumble. They could see no way that Jesus could escape from the fate that now seemed to be pressing in on him. As if it were not enough that he had prophesied his own death, he also had the powers of the authorities to face. They didn't know which was worse: the jealousy and worry of the Jewish leaders or the fragile egos of the Roman masters who wanted no-one to challenge their authority and had decided Jesus was involved with a plot to overthrow them.

Jesus was not struggling and the soldiers had no trouble leading him along.

There was no basis in law for what they were doing. No-one had produced a valid arrest warrant. No-one had laid a formal charge. It was virtually mob rule. The Jewish law enforcers were almost overwhelmed by the crowd and were having difficulty in preventing Jesus from being attacked by them. It seemed as though the whole of Jerusalem had turned against him. And it was not at all clear why.

He was not even taken to any official court or prison. Instead they made their way in the dark to the palace of the High Priest, Annas, father-in-law to Caiaphas, the one who had already said it would be better for one man to perish than put the whole of the Jewish race at risk. There was little doubt this was to be an unfair trial.

Peter and Philip followed silently, unobserved among the crowd that was jostling the soldiers. When they arrived at Annas's palace, the soldiers and Jesus went in. Philip had visited Annas a number of times and the guards at the door knew him and let him in too. Peter stayed outside, wondering what was going on. He was fighting a battle with himself. Part of him wanted to be in there, watching and supporting his master. The other part simply wanted to run.

He was not allowed the choice. The gates opened suddenly and

Philip reappeared. He had spoken to one of the women who kept the gate and persuaded her that Peter should come in too. He beckoned him in. Peter could not escape.

In the courtyard beyond the gate it was freezing cold. Annas and Jesus and the leaders of the Jews were inside the palace itself; this was as near as Peter and Philip could get.

There was a small collection of people in the courtyard, huddled around a fire they had lit to help keep themselves warm. There were a number of servants, a few officers of the guard, a few soldiers. All pressed as close as they could to the fire. Peter slid himself in among them, holding his hands out to the flames and the warming coals.

He had become separated from Philip who was now nowhere to be seen. Perhaps as an acquaintance of Annas he had been admitted to the palace itself. After looking round for him, Peter concentrated on getting warm and tried to put thoughts of running away out of his mind. He had never been in such a place before; close to the holders of power among the Jewish faith. As a humble country-dwelling Galilean more used to hills and animal tracks, the grandness of the palace overawed and overwhelmed him. He tried to look inconspicuous.

It did not work.

One of the servant girls thought she recognised him.

"You're one of his disciples, aren't you? Aren't you one of Jesus's men?"

The feeling of fear was overcoming him again and he said the only thing he could think of.

"I am not."

He moved away from her, mingled again with the small crowd and pressed forward towards the fire.

But he was not to get away with it so easily.

Another of the servants also thought she knew him and was not to be put off so easily. She called across the crowd to Peter: "Look at him – he was with Jesus of Nazareth".

He was petrified and swore loudly so that all could hear. "I was not; I do not know the man."

Despite the cold he walked away from the fire, hoping they would leave him alone. But they were too interested now. Anyone connected with Jesus was connected with what was happening that night and, unable to know what was going on inside the palace, they pursued his follower instead. And they were not going to take his no for an answer.

They followed him to the corner of the courtyard, by now certain who he was and determined to find out what they could. One of them had an unarguable point: "You *are* one of his men, your speech tells us. Anyone with a rough country voice like that comes from Galilee. You are one of them. You cannot pretend you are not".

Peter was both fearful and furious.

He swore again, wishing to the bottom of his heart he had never come in.

"I have told you. *I do not know the man.*"

But they all knew otherwise and stood quietly watching him.

Then the silence was broken with the sound of a cock crowing. And Peter remembered what Jesus had said, "Before the cock crows, you will deny me three times."

He ran. He ran and sobbed, pushing his way through the crowd, bursting out through the gate. He ran into the night, knowing he had lost everything and cursing himself for his weakness.

Once you were a High Priest, you were always called a High Priest, even though you may not be *the* High Priest of the moment.

Annas had been *the* High Priest some fifteen years previously until removed from office by the Romans. He had been seen as someone who was a little too close to the Jews and a little too far away from the Romans. This was hardly surprising, since he was a senior Jew of long standing and not likely to be particularly warm to the Romans. However, this was not what the Romans were looking for; instead they put someone in place who was more politically minded and more ready to straddle the responsibilities of holding an office that paid due court to both the Jews and the Romans. To add insult to injury, the Romans instated Annas's son-in-law, Ciaiphas, who was married to his daughter.

This had rankled with Annas ever since. In retrospect he had come to the conclusion he had been less than wise in his attitude to the Romans, and ever after had been looking for a way to ingratiate himself again with the foreign leaders. This seemed like a good opportunity.

Although he still bore the full title, he was actually now a deputy High Priest and also a member of the Sanhedrin, the supreme judicial and administrative council of the Jews.

So it was to Annas, looking for a way to please the Romans, that Jesus was taken first after his arrest in the garden of Gethsemane.

Annas's house was large; large enough to be called a palace. Inside, the rooms were vast and included one known as the court room. Some members of the Sanhedrin were already there, waiting for the troublemaker to be brought in and hoping to achieve a quick end to the difficulties he was causing. Even more importantly, they wished to prevent anything worse happening in the future.

Annas wouldn't have chosen night-time for such a confrontation but he did not want to miss an opportunity. He was old and tired. But this preliminary hearing was a wonderful chance to demonstrate that he still had power and influence over Caiaphas. He took his task seriously. If he could find any way of helping to convict Jesus, he would.

It was not a formal occasion. The senior priests and elders of the Sanhedrin who were present sat around on convenient chairs. Jesus, still bound, stood before Annas, who was seated on a high chair. A few servants and guards hovered at the back of the large room. No-one was present to look after Jesus's interests, other than himself.

Annas started by asking Jesus about the disciples.

"Who are these people you call your disciples?"

If he had hoped for a useful answer from Jesus he was disappointed.

"My disciples are those who follow me."

This was no more than the truth, since that was the definition of the word disciple. Annas had hoped for more.

"What do they want to do? What are they aiming to achieve?"

Again he was disappointed by the answer.

"They want to do what I want to do." It was Jesus's way, heard over and over again in other things he had said. Answer by repeating the question, or rephrasing the question, or turning it back on the questioner.

Annas had to press harder. He knew what he wanted to hear and tried to put words into Jesus's mouth. "It is said you want to overthrow the present order."

Jesus said, "I do".

This was better. This sounded like an admission. Annas pressed harder.

"You want to overthrow the Jewish court. Perhaps to lead a revolt against the Roman rule? To establish a new order of the Jews?"

Jesus was not to be caught that easily. "Is that what you think?"

"It is not just what I think. It is what I have heard; it is what the Jewish elders and leaders have heard. It is what the *Romans* have heard."

Jesus stayed silent.

Annas continued. "Is it not true you have zealots in your midst? Isn't Simon the Canaanite among your disciples and is he not known to be a troublemaker and one who wants to fight the established order?"

"Many people would like to fight the established order, as has been the case throughout all generations. It is not illegal to *want* to do something. Have you some proof that any of my disciples have led an attack against the Jews? Against their own faith?"

Annas had no answer to this and changed his argument.

"And what about what you teach? Are you not seeking to change the established order by words? Are you not preaching about change? About forgiveness of sinners?"

Despite his easy way of deflecting incriminating questions, Jesus was getting a little tired. Like Annas he was finding the late hour a trial in itself. Also, unlike Annas, he was facing the most extreme test of his life. And he knew he was close to an apocalyptic moment. In a way, even though he was not about to incriminate himself, he wanted to force things forward.

He answered, "I have spoken openly to the world. I have many times taught in the synagogue and in the temple where it is open to all Jews to hear me. I have said nothing in secret."

In the face of this, Annas felt himself growing exasperated. Tired, he repeated the question: "Are you not seeking to change the established order?"

Also in exasperation, Jesus replied harshly, "Why are you asking me? Ask those who heard me. They will tell you, if you don't believe me."

The words had come out strongly, more strongly than perhaps Jesus had intended. They sounded rude.

One of the officers of the guard stood forward and struck Jesus about the face with the flat of his hand, saying, "How dare you answer the High Priest like this!".

Jesus answered him in similar vein to the way he had replied to Annas a moment earlier: "If I have spoken evil, prove it. But if I have not, why do you strike me?"

Annas could see he was getting nowhere. Jesus was quite obviously not about to incriminate himself, and seemed to have an answer to every question, even though in reality it was a non-answer.

He threw up his arms in disgust; he wanted no more of this. His plan was not working and he needed his bed.

"Take him to the High Priest. Place him before the full Sanhedrin. Let us see if he can wriggle his way out of these questions in full court. Take him to Caiaphas."

Jesus was led away to face the might of the Sanhedrin itself, called to an emergency meeting in the middle of the night.

What Jesus needed was a counsel for the defence.

Unfortunately under Jewish law at the time there was no such office. Instead the rules governing the prosecution were very specific. The leader of the court should be neither friend nor foe. In particular, no-one should be a judge if it were known he was an enemy of the accused.

This immediately ruled the court invalid, since Ciaiphas had already publicly said he thought Jesus ought to be put to death "for the good of the Jewish race".

Had Jesus had a counsel he would have raised another matter. It was not legal for the Sanhedrin to meet and consider a capital offence at night, nor in a private house. They normally met twice a week in the surroundings of the Temple itself, in a room known as the Chamber of Hewn Stones. Neither should such a court convene on the day or night before a feast day or Sabbath.

The first hearing before Annas (unofficial), and now the second before Ciaiphas (slightly - but not much - more official) said only one thing. The Jewish leaders were panicking and wanted the problem out of the way and dealt with before anyone could stop them.

The Great Sanhedrin, although technically chiefly responsible for regulating Jewish religious life, also had another task, imposed by the Romans. It had to preserve law and order among its own people. If the Jews, or any particular party of the Jews, were seen to be doing anything which might threaten the rule of the Roman authorities, the Sanhedrin were expected to take steps to quash it.

The Great Sanhedrin consisted of seventy one people; the odd number so that there could never be an equal vote. All were men, fathers of families, and had to be priests, elders or scribes. More significantly, most were either Pharisees or Sadducees and served in some kind of opposition to each other.

The Sadducees were priests who came from Jerusalem's wealthiest families and concerned themselves with the running of the temple and all its religious attitudes. They did not believe in the whole idea of a Messiah sent by God: one reason why they did not approve of Jesus and what was believed about him. Also, determined to hold on to their wealth and position they co-operated with the Romans; this did not make them exactly popular with the ordinary people. It was the Sadducees therefore who were determined to extinguish any possible insurrections Jesus might inspire and find a way to condemn him before the Romans started to lean on them.

Ciaiphas was a Sadduccee, appointed by the Roman governor to ensure their influence over the Sanhedrin. It did not lead to a balanced council.

The Pharisees on the other hand as religious teachers rather than politicians were considerably more popular. Also unlike the Sadducees they believed both in the idea of a God-sent Messiah and life after death - provided God's laws were followed. They tried to keep as far away from the Roman authorities as possible. Some said that Jesus himself was a Pharisee; certainly he was often in conversation with them about Jewish beliefs.

All members of the Sanhedrin would have already served as members of lower Jewish courts, often the Small Sanhedrin, a provincial court. For a hearing to be official, there had to be twenty three members present. This was not difficult during an ordinary daytime session. But in the middle of the night, in someone's own house, this was less easy. The fact that nearly thirty were present told a story itself: the Sadducees were in a majority among those present and determined to get their desired outcome whatever it took.

They lounged about the room, gathered in a semi-circle, resting on pillows or the carpet, as was their usual custom. Jesus, still bound, was brought in, to face the next stage in the most unfair trial in human history.

CHAPTER 7

THE SECOND TRIAL: CIAIPHAS

Ciaiphas, anxious to keep the Romans happy, sat on a high chair on a slightly raised dais.

Jesus stood before him, his arms bound, making no attempt to free himself or escape.

At the back of the room stood a number of unidentified people, waiting.

Ciaiphas opened the proceedings, immediately throwing official procedures to the winds, which stated that the supreme judge of the council should not speak but only listen and arrive at a final verdict. Straightaway it became clear that this was not an examination to reach a reasonable and unbiased conclusion, but simply a means to an end. Jesus was to be found guilty - of something - and to be sentenced to death.

"We are here to try you. And have witnesses who will speak against you, that you have offended against the laws of this nation and must pay the due penalty. Who is to speak first?"

There was a shuffling at the back of the room, and then, rather too quickly, a man stepped forward. No-one asked who he was, and he volunteered nothing about himself. He spoke formally.

"I testify against this man."

"Saying?"

"He said that the Sadducees were nothing but pawns of the Romans and should be treated as enemies of the Jews."

Ciaiphas repeated the accusation, speaking slowly, loudly and clearly so that there could be no doubt as to what had been said: "*The Sadducees... should be treated as enemies.* And the next witness."

A second man, clearly ready for his moment of glory, stepped quickly forward and spoke.

"He has said that this court... this council... should be ignored, for he does not believe it is legal."

As before, Ciaiphas repeated this assertion: "*The Sanhedrin is not legal.* And the next witness."

A third man came forward. It was becoming clear the

proceedings were rehearsed.

"He says that he is above us. That he is more important than any man on earth. That he is of God."

Ciaiphas again: *"He is more important than any man.* And another witness."

A fourth man stood forward.

"I say he is an imposter. He claims to be a great prophet but he is just an ordinary man, like any of us."

"He is an imposter."

A fifth man spoke. "He is trying to overthrow the Roman rule. I have heard him say we must fight the Romans and overthrow them."

"We must fight the Romans and overthrow them."

A sixth man: "He says he can forgive sins."

"He can forgive sins. Only God can do that." Ciaiphas looked around the court. He was well satisfied with the answers he was getting. Taken together, he considered that they would incriminate any man who professed to be a dutiful member of his race.

"I think we have heard enough. This man must not be allowed to cause further trouble. We will pass sentence on him."

Ciaiphas looked round the court again, as if daring anyone to disagree.

Inconveniently, someone did.

Joseph, of the Jewish city of Aramathea, was uneasy. He had frequently been at odds with the Sanhedrin and never agreed with their single-minded determination to persecute Jesus. He had kept quiet for days and weeks before now - partly through fear, partly because he did not want to stir up trouble. But now he felt he had to speak.

"I must ask - have you forgotten the codes of the court? We cannot condemn this man on what we have just heard. It does not conform to the rules of trial."

"In what way?" Ciaiphas knew perfectly well what was being referred to, but with a majority in the court he knew he would have his way.

An elderly Pharisee clambered to his feet to support Joseph. He was old and it was difficult for him. But he was respected and no longer cared what the Sadduccees thought of him.

Slowly he spoke, his voice cracked with age. "You know the rules of trial. Witnesses must agree. If we cannot find a topic on which the witnesses agree we must stand the trial down. So far we have six statements, none of which agrees with the other – and all from people we do not know. The very first thing we must do is examine these witnesses and establish that they are true and honest men among Jews. This is all happening too fast. Let us get this court in order before we even consider arriving at a verdict."

Then, before Ciaiphas could think of an argument to quieten these two dissidents down, another man stood up.

Ciaiphas swore to himself. He knew this man. He was called Jehubabel, was a Jew, was well versed in the law, and was for ever causing trouble. How he had managed to get into the room was a mystery, but that was typical of the man. Always there when he was not wanted, always ready with a learned and annoying question. Not for the first time Ciaiphas wished he had found some way to eliminate this pest. But Jehubabel was clever: never saying something for which he could be punished, always backing up his opinions with knowledgeable and irrefutable arguments. Ciaphas waited for trouble.

"I speak," Jehubabel said slowly but with authority, "as someone who has studied the laws and who believes in the sanctity of the law. As we all must, I believe in a fair trial. And it is important for us here to be sure that this is a fair trial, conducted by the rules of law. And why is this? It is not because I disagree with you, but because if the rules of law are not followed we are all open to the charge that this man has been convicted unfairly."

Ciaiphas remained silent. He could read between the lines: whatever Jehubabel was saying, he really meant that this trial should not proceed. He was clever enough to surround himself with words that covered this up so that the court could not accuse him of anything. But he was out to stop Ciaiphas in his tracks. There was nothing Ciaiphas could do but listen and hope to find answers to the questions.

Jehubabel went on. "There seems to be no defence counsel for this man?"

It was a statement, though phrased like a question. No-one answered. He continued.

"In the absence of a defence counsel, it is the rule that the court should be entirely impartial."

"This court is impartial," Ciaiphas lied.

"If that is so, I have to ask how is it that the court has managed to produce six witnesses in the middle of the night who speak against Jesus. This cannot be an accident. This must have been premeditated. Someone of this court must have identified these people and ensured they were here at this time to make these accusations. That does not seem like impartiality."

Ciaiphas looked round the court. No-one moved or attempted to answer. He could think of no reply.

Jehubabel considered this a point won. He resumed his speech.

"Continuing with the matter of impartiality. Presumably you would consider yourself – as leader of this court – impartial?"

"Of course."

"But haven't you been heard to say, 'It would be better for one man to perish than put the whole of the Jewish race at risk'? And wasn't that remark made concerning this Jesus? And if that is so, it is difficult to see how you can be seen to be impartial."

Ciaiphas scowled, furious that this remark of his should somehow have reached Jehubabel's ears. "That was a generalisation," he said weakly.

Again, Jehubabel considered it a point won. He continued.

"I think you believe this man has incriminated himself? That that is enough for him to be condemned?"

Ciaiphas felt happier. He was on stronger ground here.

"Yes, as the witnesses have said, he has made various claims which incriminate him."

"So Jesus is in effect accusing himself?"

"Indeed."

"The law states that no-one can incriminate themselves. Self-accusation is not allowed in Jewish law. It must be discounted in any judgement."

"Stop this man!" bellowed someone in the court. The cry was taken up. "Silence him." "Evict him." "Enough!"

But Ciaiphas knew he could not do this. If he was to be presiding over any sort of acceptable court he must allow some free speech.

Especially when everything that was being said had truth in it. Nevertheless he had to find a way to end this nightmare. And a thought was beginning to occur to him.

But Jehubabel was not finished. "Which of the charges are you bringing against this man?"

"I do not understand your question."

"Which charge are you bringing against Jesus? A court charge must be consistent. There seem to be five or six different ones here. Any contradictions make the proceedings invalid."

At last Ciaiphas felt he could retaliate a little. "There might be six different testimonies, but they all relate to one charge: namely that he has offended against the laws of this nation. He is charged of this and will be sentenced accordingly at the end of this session." Ciaiphas felt more confident now. His last words were made to sound like the end of the debate. He was in charge again and Jehubabel should recognise it was the moment for him to sit down.

Unfortunately Jehubabel did not see it that way.

"I must remind you that in Jewish law you cannot be tried by night, you cannot be tried on the eve of a feast day, and you cannot convicted on the same day as a trial. Two days have to elapse for the opportunity of any further evidence to emerge. This court should be suspended".

Jehubabel now sat down. He had said all he wanted to say and knew he was on dangerous ground. It would not be particular clever to antagonise the High Priest, however right he was. But his conscience was clear; he had made his points.

For a moment Ciaiphas was lost. He paused, looking round the room. Another witness came to his aid.

The witness, one Yigal, stood up. "There is another matter oh High Priest which I feel you should hear and which does service to this court and its views. I have heard this man speak - speak treason to our race and our beliefs. He said that he himself was able to destroy the temple of God that was made by hands..." The sounds of gasping and outrage in the room swallowed up his words for the moment. And then he went on, "But - that he could rebuild it in three days *without hands*. If that is not blasphemy..." He did not trouble to finish that sentence but went on, "This is not only a constitutional offence against the law, but attacks the bedrock of our beliefs. If the temple is destroyed... there could be no greater catastrophe."

Ignoring the fact that this was yet another accusation, Ciaiphas turned to his prisoner and asked for a response. Jesus said not a word.

Instead Jehubabel stood up again. "I do not believe this was meant literally. And I do not believe it could ever be proven so. I believe Jesus was only saying that no work of man will last for ever. Unlike works of God. I was there at the time and what was said was quite different: Jesus actually said, 'You see these great buildings? Not one stone will be left upon another. All will be thrown down.' And of course he is right. In time all buildings decay and fall down. As for him rebuilding it in three days *without hands*... well, consider this. Jesus was not referring to the temple of worship at all. He was referring to the temple of the body. He was saying that even when it perishes, it will be reborn again – and not by man. Can you prove this was not what he meant?"

It sounded far-fetched to Ciaiphas but of course he could prove no such thing. Fury was rising within him; he seemed to be getting nowhere. He decided the moment had come for attack. Leaving behind the intellectual arguments he stood and stared directly at Jesus, who looked quietly back.

"You have been accused of blasphemy. What do you say?"

Jesus said nothing.

"You answer nothing? Do you take no account of what these witnesses have said? Have you no words to say to defend yourself? Do you say *nothing*?"

Jesus said nothing.

Becoming desperate, Ciaiphas finally asked the direct question, the one that *must* incriminate him. "Are you the Christ? The son of the Blessed?"

At last Jesus replied, but as so often not with a direct answer. "If I tell you, you will not believe me. And if I ask you what you mean by all this, you will not tell me, neither will you let me go."

Ciaiphas took a deep breath and embarked on his ultimate question: the question he had already asked, but said with such finality this time that everyone knew there was no going back from this moment. "I charge you under penalty by the living God that you tell this court if you are the Messiah, the Christ, the Son of God."

Jesus was beginning to have had enough. Like the others from the hills around Galilee he could be impetuous and hot-headed. And perhaps he realised he would have to answer in order to move towards the conclusion he already knew was inescapable.

"That is what you say." He started by following his usual route of never really answering the question. But his emotional Galilean temperament was taking over. He was tired; tired because it was the middle of the night, tired because this second trial was taking its toll on him. And tired of defending himself.

He took a deep breath and sealed his own fate. "I am. And you will see me, the Son of man, sitting on the right hand of God in the clouds of heaven."

It was enough.

Ciaiphas had achieved his end; they had all heard Jesus claim to be the Son of God, the Christ. Conveniently they all forgot that many prophets had claimed to be the Messiah before, and that they had never been prosecuted. It was not a criminal offence to claim to be a Messiah. Indeed, ancient writings claimed that God had declared that a kingly descendant of the House of David was indeed his Son. But this was not on today's agenda.

Ciaiphas decided he had proved his point and that what he had wanted to do all the time could now be declared.

"We need no further witnesses. We have heard for ourselves the words of his own mouth. You have all heard the blasphemy. What do you say?"

It was a clever move. It smoothly slipped straight past all the points that had been made against the trial and allowed the voices in the room - the vast majority of which Ciaiphas knew supported him - to give their verdict.

And indeed the court answered, "He is guilty and should be put to death".

In accordance with custom Ciaiphas then tore his own clothes and said formally, "He is guilty of blasphemy and is condemned to death".

The crowd in the courtroom now repeated his words and jeered at Jesus. The guards came forward and blindfolded him.

One spat on him; another struck him on the face and taunted

him: "Go on then oh prophet, oh Christ. Prophesy. Who struck you around the face?"

Jesus said nothing, as he had so often said nothing before.

The crowd at the back of the room, whipped into a sort of mass hysteria, now wanted death. The traditional method of death for blasphemy was stoning and that was what they expected. But Ciaiphas knew this could not be; at least not yet. It was one thing for the supreme Jewish court to find someone guilty and even pass sentence of death. But under the laws of Rome, the Jews were not allowed to carry out the death sentence. It needed ratification by the Roman judiciary. Ciaiphas had to turn Jesus over to the Romans. He had known this all along; it had been in his mind when the argument had seemed to be going against him. And by formally handing Jesus over to the Governor of Judea it very slightly exonerated him and his Jewish court from taking the final step against one of their own.

And there was another advantage to Ciaiphas in doing this. He would be demonstrating once again to the Roman authorities how he was doing his part in working with them to keep his people under control. And he was tacitly reinforcing the final authority of the Romans. If the Jewish people had really grasped this piece of political chicanery they might not have agreed quite so readily with Jesus's accusers.

Ciaiphas spoke his last words to the crowd in the courthouse. "We will take the accused to Pontius Pilate. We have passed our sentence and will deliver him to Rome, accused of blasphemy and treason. Then shall we see justice done."

The room was in uproar. Many of those present felt cheated of the final outcome, expecting death to be put into motion there and then, and called out in remonstration. More of the guards and even the servants shouted insults to Jesus, more of them struck him, more continued to taunt him, again asking him to prophesy who was striking him.

Still blindfolded and tied up, Jesus was pulled through the jostling crowd and led away to spend the rest of the night in a cold cell, waiting for the light of the next day and his confrontation with the Roman governor of Judea.

CHAPTER 8

THE THIRD TRIAL: PONTIUS PILATE

But the event was not quite over.

Lurking at the back of the crowd outside, his face hidden by the cowl of his robe, was Judas Iscariot. He saw Jesus led away, blindfolded and tied. He knew that even though Pilate had yet to pass judgement on Jesus, he was as good as condemned and dead. Ciaiphas would not have sent him on to the Roman Procurator if he had not been sure of the outcome. Ciaiphas and Pontius Pilate worked closely together; however different their positions, their aims were much the same when it came to political and religious unrest. It had to be stopped.

Judas saw the crowd jeering at Jesus.

And Judas repented.

What have I done? he asked himself. My beloved master; I have betrayed him. Perhaps I did it for the best of motives, but what I have actually done is commit my master to certain death. Does anything justify that? Does my desire for things to move faster, for the Kingdom of Heaven to arrive sooner, really justify having my master put to death? Haven't I just been utterly selfish, putting my own desires before anything else?

And as he asked himself the questions, he knew the answer.

And Judas repented.

He stood, watching the soldiers marching Jesus off to the cell, and wondered what to do. He argued with himself through the long hours of the night and finally arrived at a decision.

Early the following morning he made his way to the temple where he knew he would find the Chief Priests and Elders. Pushing his way forwards he found Ciaiphas in talks with the other elders, still discussing the event of the night before. Ciaiphas looked at him in astonishment. Was he after more money? If so, he certainly was not going to get it. A bargain was a bargain and that was the end of the business.

But Judas had something else to say. At first he could not start, so emotional did he feel. But eventually he got some words out.

"I have made a terrible, terrible, mistake. I have betrayed my master. I have sinned by betraying an innocent man." He fumbled in his robe and produced the bag in which the thirty pieces of silver he had been paid still remained. "Here - take back the payment. Release my master. He is innocent. Please - release him and undo the wrong that is being done."

The elders exchanged glances. What was done was done and they could not possibly undo it, not after the trial that had just ended. The man was committed for blasphemy and that was the end of it. It was now up to the Roman governor, who was even now considering the case. And besides, they had too much to lose: the goodwill of the Romans was too important to them.

Ciaiphas looked across at the others. All shook their heads. Carefully he said, "This is nothing to us. What is done is done. The problem is yours. If you feel you have made a mistake, you have to live with that mistake".

Judas stared wildly at the High Priest, the words he had spoken burning into him. *You have to live with that mistake.*

He stared at the bag of silver in his hand, then back to the High Priest. He fumbled in the bag, took a handful of silver and threw it on the ground in front of the members of the Sanhedrin who were there. He hurled the bag down after it and ran from the temple. *You have to live with that mistake.* No he didn't.

The elders picked up the pieces of silver and wondered what to do with them.

"We cannot put them back in the temple treasury; this is blood money, money paid for murder. It would not be lawful. We must take counsel as what to do with it."

Judas ran and ran until he came to a wood he knew. He took the cord from around his waist, knotted it around his neck, threw the end over a branch and leapt down into a ditch. *He didn't have to live with that mistake.*

Days later the Jewish Counsel said, "You certainly cannot put that money back into the treasury. Do something useful with it."

The Elders talked among themselves and decided to use the pieces of silver to fund a cemetery for the homeless and those without families or money. They bought a piece of land known as Potters' Field for the purpose. From then on it was called The Field of Blood.

Over five hundred years earlier, the prophet Zachariah had written, "… they took the thirty pieces of silver, the price of him that was valued…and gave them for the potters' field".

Early in the morning after the trial at Ciaiphas's palace the guards took Jesus to Pontius Pilate, the Roman Governor of Judea. This was about the middle of his eleven year reign; coming from a wealthy and powerful Roman family, he was typical of the elite Romans – perhaps three percent of the total – whose role in life was to protect the comfortable lifestyle of that elite. A provincial troublemaker like Jesus would have to be stopped before he caused an uprising that would threaten this lifestyle.

But at the same time Pilate would prefer not to get his hands dirty. Warned that Jesus was on his way, he could foresee a big problem. If he was being asked to put down "The King of the Jews" it presumably meant he would be putting down a very popular leader with hosts of followers. And what would that lead to? Uprisings against the Romans? Bloodshed even? There had been, after all, recently much talk of unrest among the Jews and a possible threat to the Roman rule through demonstrations and even fighting. It didn't seem to be connected to this particular matter, but you never knew. One thing can lead to another, and it would better to be safe than sorry. The last thing he wanted to do was inflame the position even further. Or, worst of all, actually to ignite the flames into a full-scale uprising. That must be avoided. The statesmanlike way forward would be to remove this Jesus from the scene before he caused any more trouble. But somehow he must find a way to do so without goading the Jews into more explosive action. Rather easier said than done.

After his night in the cell Jesus was led to the Praetorium, the hall of judgment. But once there, at the great door the priests and elders came to a halt. It was Passover day, and entering such a place would mean defilement. They could not go in.

So Pilate, playing his part in keeping relations good between the Jewish leaders and his position as representative of Roman law, came out to meet them.

It was a strange sight. Pilate, his Roman aides beside him, dressed in his Roman finery, facing a bound and bedraggled speechmaker from the hills of Galilee with a multitude of Jewish priests and leaders beside him seeking "justice". He had stepped outside in deference to the Jewish holy day and was wondering what he was doing there. Why couldn't these tiresome Jews sort out their own problems? Not for the first time he was tired of the charades he had to play to keep everyone happy.

Wearily he said, "What accusations are you making against this man?" His tone of voice made it clear he was not really interested or ready just to do their will. "Why have you brought him to me?"

The spokesman for the elders did not answer directly. Instead, suspecting they might not find things going their way quite as easily as they had hoped, replied rather truculently, "If he were not a criminal, we would not be handing him over to you."

Pilate repeated, "What accusations are you making?"

One by one, the priests and elders made their points.

"This man is perverting our nation…"

"He forbids us to pay our taxes to Caesar…"

"He says he is the Christ…"

"He claims to be a king…"

Still weary of the whole problem, Pilate took the easy way out and concluded that this was nothing but a local and religious matter and one that therefore should be dealt with by the Jews themselves. It had nothing to do with Roman law. And therefore nothing to do with him. As far as he was concerned there was nothing to answer.

He spoke out: "I find no fault in this man – he has done nothing amiss according to our statutes. Take him and judge him according to your own law". He turned to go back into the court. But one of the elders called out to him.

"We have found him guilty. Our will is that sentence of death should be passed upon him. But you know the law, the Roman law as you have made it: that we Jews may not put any man to death. That is why we come to you. This man has made blasphemy against us and against you. He has said that he is King of the Jews and even prophesied that he would be killed for his beliefs. We ask that you pass this sentence of death."

Pontius Pilate could not ignore the direct request – or the

reference to Jesus having blasphemed against the Romans. He turned back, speaking to Jesus himself and beginning to wonder if after all he should take the action they were demanding of him.

"*Are* you the King of the Jews?"

"If you say so." It was Jesus's typical answer; not an answer at all.

"You have heard of what you have been accused. What do you say?"

Jesus said nothing.

Pilate listed the accusations. "What do you say to all this?"

Jesus said nothing.

Pilate was becoming exasperated. "You hear all that is said. You hear all these things that are spoken against you. Are you not going to answer? Do you *still* say nothing?"

Jesus still said nothing. In the face of this astonishing determination not to say anything or defend himself in any way, the governor was speechless himself. He decided to talk to Jesus in private, hoping that with the priests and elders not present Jesus might be more forthcoming.

"Come inside."

Jesus followed him. Inside procurator and rebel stood face to face. Pilate tried again. "Is what they say true? Do you say you are King of the Jews?"

Jesus was no more helpful inside that he had been outside, and answered, "Are you saying this for yourself, or because others are asking you?"

Pilate's response was brusque: "Am I a Jew? This is not up to me. Your own people and the Chief Priests have delivered you to me as procurator. So I ask you again, what have you done that they should bring you here? Do you still say you are the King of the Jews?"

Away from the crowd outside Jesus at last answered more directly. For the first time he spelled out his situation to someone who was neither a Jew nor a follower.

"My kingdom is not of this world."

It sounded rather mystical to Pilate, who blinked and tried to work out what it meant. He guessed that Jesus must be considering himself a spiritual leader rather than a temporal one. This must mean then that his kingdom was in heaven; the Jewish heaven. Jesus's next words seemed to confirm it.

"If my kingdom were of this world, my servants would fight to prevent me from being delivered to the Jews. But it is not. My kingdom is not of here."

Pilate considered for a moment and continued to examine exactly what Jesus meant. Finally he said, "But if you have a kingdom, somewhere, you are a king."

"As you say. And yes, that is why I was born and that is why I came into this world, that I should reveal the truth. All who recognise the truth know it is as I say." He repeated: "My kingdom is not of this world".

He seemed to be saying that to him earthly kingdoms were irrelevant, that Pilate's rule of law meant nothing, that it didn't matter to Jesus or any of those who knew the truth, what Pilate and the Romans said and did. The implication was obvious: he was above all that.

Pilate looked away. He decided not to take offence, as he might easily have done. Instead, as an intelligent man, he thought back over what Jesus had just said. "What is this truth that all should recognise?" he asked, almost to himself. Truth probably depends on who is saying it and what they believe. Jesus was making outrageous claims. But they were *religious* claims, *personal* claims.

There was no way out of this, no logical outcome from this conversation. Neither of them could come to a resolution that they both could agree with.

Eventually Pilate decided this was still a local, religious, problem.

He went back outside and repeated what he had said earlier. "I find no fault in this man."

The crowd shouted at him: "But he is stirring up the people wherever he goes. He has been causing trouble throughout all the Jewish kingdom. Right from when he was first in Galilee to here and now in Jerusalem."

Pilate pricked up his ears. He had heard something new, something which might rescue him from this mire from which he could see no way out.

"You say he is from Galilee? He is a Galilean?"

"He is, he is."

Pilate breathed a sigh of relief to himself. He would get away from all this yet without having to commit himself.

"If he is a Galilean," he said, quietly triumphant, "he does not come under my jurisdiction. He must appear before Herod Antipas, the ruler of Galilee."

Very conveniently for Pilate, Herod was actually in the city of Jerusalem as they spoke. He had travelled there to be with his subjects for the Feast of the Passover. It couldn't have worked out better.

"Take him to Herod. Let Herod decide; he is better qualified and better placed to answer this problem."

Pilate retreated inside his court, confident that he had done all he should and that he could exit from the situation with dignity.

CHAPTER 9

THE FOURTH TRIAL: HEROD ANTIPAS

As he approached Herod's palace, Jesus had mixed feelings. For all that he had said that his kingdom was above all earthly kingdoms and that it mattered not to him what the Romans - or anyone else, for that matter - decided about him, he knew he was in deep trouble. Not least because he had once compared Herod Antipas to a fox.

The son of Herod the Great, and thus a Jewish leader but not a Jew, Herod Antipas liked to imply that he was at one with his Jewish subjects. It was typical that he should have travelled to Jerusalem to be with them for the celebration of the Passover. But Jesus had never been persuaded that Antipas's interest was anything more than a ploy and thus he had publicly said he was a fox, an animal ritually considered unclean.

The Jews had another problem with Herod Antipas. Willed by his father to be tetrarch of Galilee and Peraea (the east bank of the Jordan), he had been confirmed in this position by the emperor Augustus. To demonstrate his loyalty to the great Roman empire, Antipas had built a new capital city in honour of the emperor Tiberius. Unfortunately this had rebounded against him, for his aims were better than the actuality. Shortly after the construction was complete, it was discovered that he had built the city over an ancient Jewish graveyard. This had not endeared him to his Jewish subjects.

Despite all this, Antipas himself was interested to meet Jesus. Jesus was probably less interested in meeting him, since Antipas's father, Herod the Great, had tried to kill Jesus at birth, along with all the other small children in Bethlehem.

But that was a long time in the past. Today Jesus had an even stronger argument with Antipas: the murder of his cousin John the Baptist.

The background to this was Antipas's complicated private life. Divorcing his first wife, Phasaelis, he then married the confusingly-named Herodias. She had previously been the wife of Antipas's half-brother (also called Herod). She was also the daughter of another half-brother, Aristobulus (who shared this name with Herod the Great's former chief of staff). Thus Antipas was married to someone who was both his sister-in-law and his niece.

John the Baptist had earlier proclaimed the coming of the Messiah and baptised his cousin Jesus in the river Jordan. At the same time he had also publicly criticised Antipas for what he had described as his immoral private life. Antipas felt under much pressure to eliminate the Baptist and stop these public criticisms. But equally he knew how popular the Baptist was and feared the effect it would have if he put him to death. While wondering what to do about this he received an unexpected impetus from his daughter, Salome.

This high-spirited young lady delighted in dancing in public, slowly removing a number of veils as she did so. So thrilled was Antipas at these displays that at the end of one particularly enthralling performance he promised her any present she would choose. Her request was the head of John the Baptist on a plate. Caught, he had to oblige and straightaway put Jesus's cousin to death.

Jesus therefore approached the palace of Herod Antipas with a very clear view of his next judge.

Jesus did not go alone to Herod. Along with the soldiers accompanying him, a number of the priests and elders of the Temple went too, to see justice done.

Herod Antipas had not needed much encouraging to see Jesus. He had heard all about him and his preaching and the miracles he was famous for. Moreover, he hoped that Jesus would demonstrate a miracle especially for him. Conveniently ignoring their past history, he expected Jesus to perform upon command.

But first he had duties to carry out.

He repeated the accusations of Annas, Ciaiphas and Pilate and asked if they were all true. As had happened so often during these trials, Jesus made no reply.

A little disconcerted, Antipas asked more specifically, "Are you the Christ?"

No reply.

"Do you say you are the Son of God?"

No reply.

"Do you incite people to overthrow Roman rule?"

No reply.

"Do you tell people not to pay their taxes?"

No reply.

Herod was becoming annoyed. This man was clearly not going to engage in any sort of conversation or interplay with him. He became more sharp.

"You are a blasphemer." No question this time, but a charged statement. The result was the same: no reply.

He tried one last time. "You think the Jewish law is above that of the Romans." Again a charged statement; again receiving no reply.

At a loss, Herod looked for help to the Jewish elders assembled before him. They too tried to get some response from Jesus, repeating their accusations. But Jesus remained stubbornly silent.

Now Herod had had enough. He gestured his annoyance to the guards and servants, giving them permission to do and say what they liked to this irritating preacher. Feeling that he was mocking their beliefs, the Roman guards took the opportunity to make fun of him.

They danced around him, calling obscenities at him. They threw fruit and stones at him. They mocked him as though he really were a king. Then one had a bold idea, disappeared for a few moments, reappeared with a crimson robe, which they tied around him. Now he *looked* like a king. Sinking to their knees before him they pretended obeisance. Yet through everything they did, he remained the same: ignoring them, not responding to their words, not reacting to their actions. At last Herod had had his fill of this rather disappointing game.

"Send him back to Pilate. I want nothing further to do with this man. This is a problem for the Jews, not for us."

So Jesus was returned to the Roman Procurator who had, after all, to make the final decision.

Oddly, this strange business had reunited Pilate and Herod, who had been at odds with each other for some years. In face of this inconvenient upstart and his supporters, they found themselves in agreement for once.

CHAPTER 10

THE FIFTH TRIAL: PONTIUS PILATE

Warned by messenger that Antipas was returning Jesus to him after all, Pilate decided the nettle had to be grasped and the matter settled once and for all. And given the huge interest the whole affair was now generating, it had to be done publicly and visibly: the Jews in particular had to understand that this whole business had gone far enough and that the Romans were not to be trifled with.

Accordingly he had the stage set for a public final act.

Outside his palace was an esplanade, a sort of wide pavement; an ideal place for a gathering and a judgment. It was to be a great tableau, a set piece of Roman law in action.

Pilate sat there on a raised throne in all his glory; his most extravagant garments around him, determined to appear strong and statesmanlike. Around him, his guards and servants, presenting a unified front of power.

Before him, a figure almost of farce. Still dressed in the mock finery draped around him by Herod's guardsmen, and with smears of blood on his face and body, stood the slight form of an irritating preacher from the provinces. It was an uneven match.

Beyond the esplanade and facing the might of Pilate and his guard stood – or rather writhed – the mass of the Jews who had by now raised themselves into a great state of excitement. Fearing that the Romans might take this opportunity to beat them into submission again to quell the feeling of revolt that was in the air, they had decided to sacrifice Jesus to them. *Better that one man should die than a whole race suffer.* They perhaps did not realise it, but in crying for Jesus's death they would indeed be making him their saviour.

Pilate however, and for all his brave front, was wrestling with a number of difficulties. And no doubt these very difficulties were contributing to his determination to appear strong and decisive.

The first problem was his wife. They had heard in the early hours that Jesus was to be returned to them from Herod. Pilate's wife Herodias had then slipped into an uneasy sleep, during which she had experienced an inconvenient dream. Herod had left her asleep and gone forth to meet Jesus. And while he was sitting there a messenger arrived and handed him a small section of papyrus. On it was a message from Herodias.

"Have nothing to do with this man," she had written. "I have suffered many things in a dream because of him."

Pilate looked at this missive with some irritation. Life was hard enough without the confusion of an instruction from his wife based on no more than a bad dream. The trouble was that deep down Pilate knew he was stuck in something of a nightmare himself. He would have liked little more than to have nothing to do with this man. But it could not be. The drama was moving on and there was nothing he could do to stop it. He had to go forward, despite the quite legitimate forebodings of his wife.

The other big problem, as ever, was striking the right balance between Jewish and Roman interests. His real responsibility was to maintain calm and prevent friction between the two. But doing this without seeming to offer preferment to one or the other was a permanent problem. No wonder he had hoped to transfer to the problem to Herod Antipas.

Once Pilate was satisfied everyone was there who ought to be there – the Chief Priests and elders, as well as the jeering crowd – he spoke to the throng, making one final attempt to avoid trouble.

"You have caused this man to be brought to me as someone who is perverting the people. But hear me; I have already examined this man in front of you. You know I have found no fault in him concerning those things you accuse him of. Not even the king Herod could find any fault. He could find nothing worthy of the penalty of death. I am therefore going to release this Jesus – but first I will chastise him. He must learn his lesson. He will be beaten so that he will know to cause no trouble in the future. And then he will be released."

It was a dangerous strategy. Pilate said what he wanted to say and hoped to take the crowd with him. A good beating would teach Jesus to control himself and make no more difficulties for the ruling parties. That done, and tough honour satisfied, he could be released and all would be over. Hopefully the crowd would be satisfied with that. The danger was that they would not see it that way. They might want more decisive action. If that were the case, Pilate, as a true politician, had a neat alternative up his sleeve.

It did not take long to see how the land lay.

"Away with this man," they cried.

"I have said what I have said," said Pilate. "I find no fault in him."

The response was swift and decisive.

"Crucify him! Crucify him!"

Pilate embarked on his alternative strategy. "You have a custom. At the Passover we release one prisoner to you. One man shall go free. Let us follow your custom. Let me release one man. And let that man be the King of the Jews."

This was met by confusion. For a moment there was silence, then a great commotion burst out, as Jew argued with Jew and the Romans allowed themselves a little sport by raising their voices too.

Eventually the Chief Priests and elders took control; again the crowd called for the death of Jesus.

Pontius Pilate replied by giving them a choice. "All right. Whom do you choose to be released? Jesus, King of the Jews? Or Barabbas, the murderer?"

Barabbas, the crowd knew, was a convicted killer who had been charged with taking part in an uprising against the Romans earlier that year. It would suit Pilate to have Barabbas put to death; certainly as far as the Romans were concerned it was infinitely more appropriate.

Unfortunately there was a problem of identity here. Barabbas's full name, as most of the crowd were aware, was Jesus Barabbas. And Barabbas was not a name at all but a description or title. Bar meant "son of" and Abba "father". Its usual usage however was "Father"; in other words, God. Thus the crowd was being offered the choice between Jesus, King of the Jews, and Jesus, Son of God. Even more complicated: both Jesus's were apparently guilty of insurrection against the Romans.

Who to condemn to death? The kingly Jesus or the Godly Jesus?

The Jewish crowd were clear; they wanted to save Barabbas. He was much less well-known. He was causing less trouble. He wasn't claiming to be a king. He was less likely to cause the Romans to set about crushing them. But for ever after the question remained: who was the *real* Jesus? Those who have said that Jesus was not hanged on a cross were just as right as those who said he was.

Again Pilate said, "Whom shall I release to you? Barabbas? Or Jesus who is called Christ?"

The crowd knew who they wanted.

"Send us Barabbas."

"Away with this man Jesus."

"Let him be destroyed."

It was still the wrong answer for Pilate. Barabbas was already a convicted felon; there was no argument that he was guilty and should be put to death. Jesus, on the other hand, didn't appear to be guilty at all. Pilate had yet another try.

"Who shall I release to you? Jesus, the Christ?"

But the crowd were determined. "Crucify him. Crucify him."

"But why? He has done no evil."

The Chief Priests, who – as Pilate well knew – were determined to have Jesus condemned because they felt threatened by him, moved among the people. Already carried along by their own shouting, they needed little encouragement to stay with their original intent.

"Jesus! Crucify Jesus!"

Pilate was not giving up that easily. He repeated what he had said earlier, in one last hope they would go along with it. "I have found no cause of death in him. I will chastise him and let him go. Let that be enough."

It wasn't. The crowd cried out even louder and Pilate began to fear that things might get out of hand. He gave in.

With a wave of his hand he indicated to the guards that Barabbus should be set free. But any belief that that might be the end of the affair quickly vanished. Barabbus disappeared into the crowd with no-one appearing to be particularly interested in him. They wanted blood; Jesus's blood.

Pilate, who had hoped to be able to leave the scene and allow the sentence of death to take its course without him, found he could not walk away. The crowd were still chanting; all waiting to see their version of justice done.

A streak of stubbornness in Pilate made him take his next course of action.

"Water!" he called.

His servants brought him a pail of water.

Ceremoniously and visibly, he washed his hands. As he did so, very deliberately he said, "I am innocent of the blood of this just person. The blood is not upon me, but on you."

They didn't care. They were proud of their decision and shouted back, "Yes – the blood is on us, and our children".

It was traditional before a crucifixion to scourge the victim, symbolically cleansing him of all evil before committing him to the next life. It was not pretty, yet something crowds seemed to enjoy.

Before long Jesus was covered in blood from the whipping around his face and body.

Then Pilate's soldiers took Jesus out of sight of the crowd, into the great hall of Pilate's palace and started to make fun of him. They took away the clothing he had on and wrapped a ceremonial robe around him. They plaited a crown of thorns and set it upon his head. They pushed a reed into his right hand. And then they mocked him. Bowing to worship and going down on bended knees, they called, "Hail, King of the Jews!". Then they spat upon him and hit him around the head with their hands.

Pilate made yet another attempt to disassociate himself from the proceedings. Coming back onto the esplanade and taking his seat on the judgment throne he said to the crowd, "See – I bring him forth to you again that you should know I find no fault in him".

He beckoned for Jesus to be brought out, still wearing the ceremonial robe and the crown of thorns and with blood upon him. Jesus stood still and in silence before the multitude.

Pilate said simply, "Behold the man".

As soon as they saw Jesus, the crowd raised their voices even higher: "Crucify him! Crucify him!"

Knowing he had little alternative and furious at being told what to do, Pilate replied, "Take him. *You* take and crucify him. You know I find no fault in him".

Angry that he was still defending Jesus, the crowd answered back. "We have our law, and by our law he should die."

And, "He has called himself the Son of God and that is blasphemy. He should die."

Becoming alarmed by the pressure from the crowd, Pilate turned to Jesus and tried to get answers from him again.

"Is it true? Where are you from? From whom are you born?"

But, as so often, Jesus made no reply.

Becoming ever more irritated, Pilate tried again. "Do you not speak to me? Do you not know I have both the power to crucify or release you?"

At last Jesus responded. "You have no power over me at all. You could only have power over me if you had the power from above. I am no sinner; the real sinner here is the one who brought me to you."

The words alarmed Pilate who felt himself more and more in the wrong, but unable to extricate himself from the situation he found himself in. He tried again to get the crowd to allow Jesus to go but they were having none of it.

They cried out, "If you let him go, you are no friend of Caesar. For if you let him say he is a king he is a rival to Caesar; he is a rebel."

Pilate found that argument impossible to refute. And whatever he might think himself, if someone passed this view on to Caesar Pilate himself would be in dire trouble.

So he gave in. It was about noon of the day of preparation for the Passover and Pilate had had enough.

Wearily he said, "Here is your king".

"Take him away, crucify him," they yelled.

"What – crucify your king?" It was a last vain attempt to head them off.

"We have no king but Caesar," said the Chief Priests, not meaning it but determined to have Jesus's head. Pilate made a gesture of acceptance of their wishes. "Take him. Take him," he said and left the seat of judgment. He had lost.

The soldiers untied Jesus, stripped him of his ceremonial robe and crown of thorns and put his own clothes back on again. They took little care, and he looked a pathetic sight. Still streaked with blood on his face and shoulders, scratches around his temple from the crown of thorns, his garments thrown casually around him, it would be hard for anyone to believe he could possibly be a king of anyone.

Silent as ever he accepted it as bravely as anyone could after what he had already been through.

Beyond the palace a cross was already waiting. If not Pilate, then certainly the Roman soldiers and servants had guessed what would be the outcome of the trial. In any case it was their duty to be ready for any eventuality.

It was not uncommon to expect a convicted criminal to carry his own cross.But the cross was large and heavy. It had to be strong enough to carry the weight of a man; it had to be tall enough to take his full height. Looking at the sight of the bedraggled, injured and exhausted Jesus, it was hard to see how he could manage his task.

It seemed he was to get no help.They stood him before the cross and waited. Not complaining, not speaking, he tried. He pushed his tired body beneath the arms of the cross and tried to straighten himself up. For a moment the heavy wooden cross was off the ground, but Jesus could not maintain the lift and it dropped again, falling on top of him.

"Again," said the leaders of the body of soldiers roughly. "Get on with it, we have a way to go."

Jesus raised the cross again and began to stagger slowly forward, blood and perspiration mingling on his forehead, his breath coming painfully. Step after step he took, yet seeming to be making no ground at all, the destination as far off as ever.

"Come on!" shouted the centurion, "let's get this *done.*"

Jesus tried again, managed a few more faltering steps, and came to a halt, the cross again slipping to the ground, grazing his side as it did so. More blood mingled with that already there. There were people watching who were enjoying the sight, believing that justice was being done and the right decision had been made. There were others who found that pity was the stronger emotion. No human being deserved this. Among those watching from a distance were some of his own family; that family he had disowned earlier, but now, at the end, wanting to be reunited, the blood relationship stronger than any other.

Eventually, and in the interests more of practicality than sympathy, the soldiers looked around for someone to help (it was beneath their dignity to do anything themselves).The day had started far too early and they wanted to get the boring interlude of the journey over and get on to the real business as quickly as possible. And then back to their quarters for a bit of a celebration.

Into view came a Cyrenian, one Simon. He had come in from the country that morning, and was known to some of the people gathered there as the father of two young men, Alexander and Rufus. He had seen the crowds and come across to see what was going on. He looked suitably strong.

"He'll do."

"Come on you, give us a hand here."

Simon took one look at the scene and for a split second wished he hadn't been passing at that moment. But it was too late. There were too many guards to argue, and in any case the man clearly needed help. Suddenly he realised who it was and where he was heading. He knew of Jesus and had even heard him preach. Words came back to him: "If you are asked to go one mile, go two". A natural feeling of humanity and affinity with the teachings of Jesus left Simon with little option. Silently he moved forward and raised the cross from the ground, meeting Jesus's eyes at he did so and seeing the gratitude in them.

Together they made their way forward, Jesus finding it hard to walk with his wounds and the prospect of death in front of him, Simon faltering under the weight of the heavy wooden cross. The guards led them on, the crowd following and surrounding them, their sounds a mixture of ebbing excitement and growing compassion. Women, in particular, were now crying out loud, the enormity of what was happening finally overtaking them.

Through his suffering Jesus heard them, stopped and faced them, calling out his last bitter words of teaching.

"Daughters of Jerusalem – do not weep for me – weep for yourselves and your children. It would be better that you and they were never born. Indeed in time to come people will say blessed are those who are barren, whose wombs have never born offspring, who have never suckled a child. People will wish that the mountains fall on them and the hills cover them rather than suffer what this world is bringing. For if they do these things to a young shoot of hope, what will they do to beliefs when they become established ?"

And then they moved on.

CHAPTER 11

CRUCIFIXION

Slowly they made their way to a place which in Hebrew was called Golgotha - "the place of a skull". Or in the Latin tongue, Calvary.

Just outside the city walls and to the north of the Damascus Gate, it was a typical crucifixion site - near a road where all could see what happened to those who challenged the Roman rule.

Golgotha was a hill; a small rocky hill, with two caves in its side. The caves looked like a pair of eye sockets in an empty skull. Which was one reason why it was called the place of a skull. The other reason was that there were a number of other skulls about: a dire warning not to cross swords with the great Roman empire.

As they arrived at Golgatha it became apparent that Jesus was not to be crucified alone; two other crosses were already erected. They stood no higher than a man, so that his feet could rest on the ground. People lasted much longer when crucified if they could stand on their own feet.

Both crosses were already occupied; by thieves, it was discovered later. They had not been there long; the blood was flowing from their hands where they had been nailed up. Their legs were tied closely to the bottom of the crosses. Already faint, their heads hung low, watching without much curiosity at the third man arriving to be crucified with them but wondering why there was such a crowd surrounding him.

There was a gap between them. It was clear where Jesus was heading.

Simon the Cyrenian was at the end of his tether. The cross was overwhelmingly heavy and he doubted whether he would have survived many more yards. As they arrived the soldiers roughly took it from him, allowing him to collapse on the ground, his breath rasping, his hands and shoulders grazed and bleeding from the work he had been doing.

They erected the cross between the two thieves and from the ground Jesus stared at it, seeing both his death and his future looming above him.

The sounds of the crowd were growing now that they had arrived at the final stop in the journey. The Jewish elders and priests had kept

up a barrage of hostile shouts throughout the journey. The women
- and particularly the family and former close friends of Jesus who
had known him in Gallilee - were crying softly a little way off,
frightened of the Romans and of the Jews who seemed to have
turned against their one-time leader.

Only one of his disciples could be seen: John, son of Zebedee.

Jesus was pale in the face and the perspiration ran from him,
congealing with the blood from the earlier treatment he had received
from the soldiers. One appeared to take pity on him, for he offered
up a drink in a pitcher. At first Jesus seemed ready to drink, but
suddenly he turned his face away. Believing he was just refusing help
from the soldiers, the crowd fell silent for a moment. But then they
saw the soldier laughing and they guessed this was vinegar wine he
was offering; a bitter joke.

And then they began the process of crucifixion.

As they did so, Jesus said, "Father forgive them, for they know not
what they do." Was he referring to the Roman guards, who were
nailing the Son of God to the cross? Or to the Jewish elders, who had
betrayed their king? Or was he alluding to the whole of mankind,
who were despatching their saviour to the next world?

They stood him against the cross and nailed his hands to its
outstretched arms.

They tied his legs together to the bottom of the cross and nailed
them there for good measure. And then they stood back to wait for
the loss of blood to take its toll. This might take a long time. People
had been known to survive on the cross for up to three days. The
prisoners just stood there, feet brushing the ground and just
managing to take the weight of the body, blood slowly seeping from
the wounds, faintness relentlessly overcoming them from lack of food
and water. And all the time they would be taunted by passers-by or
anyone with an interest in that particular crucifixion.

Once Jesus was on the cross, the soldiers tore his outer clothing
from him. Four sections came away separately and four soldiers took
one each. But the final garment was made all of one piece, woven
from the top down without seam; a sign of good quality. Jesus could
not have been such a poor peasant, after all. It only made it the more
poignant that he was to die the death of a dissonant rebel.

"Let us not tear it," the soldiers agreed, "it's too good to split the cloth among us. We'll cast lots for it." Was it a coincidence that an ancient prophecy said, "They parted my raiment among them, and for my vesture they did cast lots"?

It was customary with a crucifixion to post some kind of charge sheet, setting out the reason for the execution so that all would know what the prisoner had been guilty of and to warn them against similar crimes.

Thus Pilate had caused an inscription to be prepared on a tablet, which was fixed upon the cross itself. In three languages, Greek, Latin and Hebrew, it said THIS IS JESUS, THE KING OF THE JEWS.

The crowd surged forward to read the superscription and the Jews started muttering among themselves. It was not what they wanted written, for it seemed to suggest that he *was* the King of the Jews – which they did not want to believe. Also it proclaimed once again the authority of the Romans, who had the power to crucify the Jewish king at will.

After much discussion, some of the elders returned to Pilate in his palace and tried to persuade him to change the inscription.

They said, "Do not put THE KING OF THE JEWS, but rather HE SAID HE WAS THE KING OF THE JEWS".

The subtlety of this change of emphasis was not lost on Pilate, who recognised the attempt of the elders to imply that it was not actually their king who was being put to death, but just someone making a false claim.

Unfortunately for them, Pilate had had quite enough of the troublesome Jesus and the even more troublesome Jewish leaders. He saw an opportunity and wasted no further time or breath.

"What I have written, I have written," he barked out. In other words, "I have no intention of changing anything; go away and let this be an end to the whole thing. And, incidentally, I might point out that since you are the instigators of all this you have made yourselves look rather absurd".

Unhappy, feeling that events had got completely out of hand and what had seemed like a good idea was now looking rather less so, the elders made their way back to Golgotha, aware that somehow the Roman leader had trumped them in the end, publicly letting it be known that they were responsible for the killing of their own king.

At Golgotha the two thieves on either side of Jesus were looking at him. They had realised by now who he was and curiosity had overcome their pain for the moment.

One of them was scornful; angry even "If you are Jesus, the Christ, save yourself - and us!"

But the other saw it differently. He retorted to the first thief: "Do you not fear God? Seeing you are condemned in the same way and are about to face your maker? Do you not see the difference between us and him? We have deserved our penalty, it is the due reward for what we have done. But this man... this man has done nothing wrong."

He turned to face Jesus directly and said, "Jesus - Lord - remember me when you come into your kingdom".

Jesus replied, "Truly, I say to you, today you will be with me in paradise".

But the sharp words of the first thief were picked up and echoed by others standing around the cross. A variety of cries went up.

"You who claimed to destroy the temple and rebuild it in three days, save yourself and come down from the cross."

"He saved others - yet he cannot save himself".

"Let Christ the King of Israel come down from the cross now so that we may see and believe."

"He trusted in God. He said he was the son of God. So let's see if God will have him and save him."

"If you are the King of the Jews, save yourself."

The cries came from the priests and the Scribes, from the Roman soldiers, from casual passers-by. Somehow the man who had been a hero, who had been a leader and a giver of hope, who had saved and revived so many others, had become an outcast, a man whose death everyone seemed to be seeking. A mass hysteria had taken over and this now pathetic-looking man had become the focus for it all.

But not all the crowd were shouting. A small group of women - and one man - who had been looking on from a distance slowly made their way forwards. They were not joining with the rest in condemning Jesus; silently they looked and wept. Three of them were called Mary: Mary, Jesus's mother; Mary Magdalene; and Mary, wife of Cleophas and the mother of James and Joses. The fourth woman was Salome, wife of Zebedee and the mother of James and John. The sole man was this same John, known to be one of Jesus's favourite disciples.

There had been little communication between Jesus and his mother since soon after he had started his public teaching. They had not supported him, and he had acted accordingly. But now their disagreements were in the past and, as any mother would be, she was there at his end.

Jesus looked upon her. Following his own teachings he would always be ready to forget and forgive, always looking forward to something that would make a better life. Even on the cross he was finding answers to difficulties. He looked from her to the disciple John and said to his mother, "Woman, this is now your son". And to John he said, "Behold your mother". The meaning was clear: "I commend you to each other, to replace me in your hearts." And from that day on, Mary went to live at John's home.

It was Jesus's final act of kindness. He had settled his mother for the rest of her life; he had given his favourite disciple something to do that would for the rest of his days remind him of the days he had spent with his master and all that he had learnt.

Now the end was here.

He said, "I am thirsty".

One of the soldiers offered him the bitter vinegar wine again, dipping a sponge in it, impaling it on a stick and holding it up to Jesus's mouth. He did it perhaps because even vinegar would quench the thirst for a moment; perhaps, for a less generous reason, because it would prolong his life a little and keep the entertainment going a little longer.

Jesus took a drop of the vinegar and then spoke a few more words. "It is finished."

It was the conclusion of his teaching and of his work on earth. He was now anticipating, in some way or other, the Kingdom of Heaven.

He fell silent. A similar peace overcame the crowd, who sensed the end was near.

And yet it was not.

It was now noon. As can sometimes happen on a day when the

sunlight never appears and the clouds hang low, the light began to fail. The crowd and the three crosses and the top of the hill became shrouded in a kind of darkness, where shapes loomed out of the gloom and a ghostly pall descended over everything.

For three hours this lasted, until the silence was broken by one cry. It came from the cross in the centre.

"Eloi, Eloi, lama sabachthani?" *My God, my God, why have you forsaken me?*

Not everyone heard this properly, or understood what he meant. Many thought Jesus was calling on the prophet Elijah, known as a miracle worker. Excitedly the crowd waited for a miracle.

But no miracle happened. Consciously or unconsciously Jesus had echoed the opening words of the twenty-second Psalm of David. It was a bitter, desolate psalm, which had other words which might just as well have been used. *Why are you so far from helping me? I cry in the daytime and you hear me not. All they that see me laugh me to scorn… saying, he trusted on the Lord that he would deliver him…* And you haven't.

Certainly Elijah did not come to the rescue. But Jesus never expected he would. He was calling on his own God, his father in heaven, whatever the people gathered there had thought.

His words made it seem as though he felt cheated at the last moment. All his teaching life he had been saying that the Kingdom of God would come. He had spent his life healing the sick and curing the soul, promising all the time that the great day was near. Had he been anticipating being saved by God's coming and now realised that it was not to be? Did it mean that he had failed the people? He who had lived in hope now appeared to be dying in despair.

Or perhaps he was just in such pain that he spoke as anyone might.

Then Jesus uttered his last words.

"Father, into your hands I commend my spirit."

It was three o'clock in the afternoon. And he died.

Three hours was not long to be alive on the cross. But it was hardly surprising that Jesus had died so soon. He had barely slept for days. He had been pursued by some of his own people, he had endured trials in both day and night, he had tried to carry his heavy cross, he had had nothing to eat or drink since the Passover meal with the disciples.

At the moment when the centurion in charge of the soldiers realised that one of his three charges had passed away the day was still dark. To some, those who still believed in him, it appeared that the darkness was total; the light of the world had gone completely out.

Others claimed more amazing things. That the hangings in the temple had been torn from top to bottom. That the earth shuddered. That rocks were moved. That graves were opened and the spirits walked forth, appearing to people throughout the city.

What was clear was that something infinitely greater had happened than just a troublesome preacher put to death.

The first person it struck was the centurion himself. A Roman, it was all the more astonishing then that he should say: "Truly this man was the Son of God... a righteous man".

Others took his lead. Amazingly, those in the crowd who only a few hours earlier had been calling for his execution now were beating their breasts. After the frenzy leading up to the crucifixion the people were having second thoughts and would regret it for the rest of their lives.

It was important for the Jews that the bodies should not be still on the crosses on the Sabbath, the following day. Bodies should be buried before sundown.

To make sure they were all dead, they sent messengers to Pilate, asking that the legs of the prisoners on the crosses should be broken. Without the support of their legs, those hanging on the cross could no longer hold themselves up and death would follow much more quickly. Then the bodies could be removed.

Tired of the whole business, Pilate consented. He sent soldiers to the hill and they duly broke the legs of the two prisoners who had been crucified with Jesus. But when they came to Jesus himself, they were surprised to find him already dead.

To prove his death beyond doubt, one of the soldiers pierced his side with a spear. With the heart stopped, no blood flowed.

Jesus was, indeed, dead.

CHAPTER 12

AN EMPTY TOMB

Like any parent, Jesus's mother Mary would have liked to have buried her son back at their family home. They were far from Galilee here; it was foreign territory and it seemed a terrible thing to leave her son behind.

There was no chance of transporting the body home and the sorrowing women who were with her tried to comfort her while they agonised over what to do. Arranging burial in a strange city was beyond them. They couldn't afford it, and they had no idea how to go about it. The alternative – being buried in a pauper's grave without ceremony or anything to mark the place – seemed inevitable. It was the saddest end to a life that had already dismayed Mary for so long.

She was not helped in her agony by the almost total absence of the disciples. She had never been impressed with them – nor the life her son had led with them – and was hardly surprised that they had deserted him when the family needed them most. Only Salome and Zebedee's son John was there. The five of them seemed to be emptily alone.

There was yet another problem facing them, and a rather gruesome one. Someone had to take the body down from the cross. And if they did not want it to be defiled further by the rough and unclean hands of the Praetorean guard, they would have to do it themselves and somehow transport it to the strangers' burial ground. Though determined to do the best they could for their son of Galilee they shuddered at the prospect

But unknown to them, help was at hand. That one member of the Sanhedrin, Joseph of the Jewish city Aramathea, who had always secretly disagreed with the proceedings of the trial and the sentence of death that had been proclaimed on Jesus, was having thoughts.

The might and power of the elders and Chief Priests had always seemed to him too forbidding to argue much against. Somehow he had screwed up the courage to stand up and make some points before the Sanhedrin, but never felt he had done enough or sounded forceful enough about something on which he really felt deeply.

Ashamed of himself, at the back of his mind he had been constantly on the look-out for an opportunity to redeem himself. And now he saw it.

Putting his usual caution and unobtrusive nature behind him, he made his way in the evening to Pilate's palace. A rich man, Joseph had no trouble in being admitted to the Governor's presence.

Pilate looked warily at Joseph. Somehow this matter of Jesus refused to go away. What now?

"I am here to beg a request," started Joseph rather hesitantly. He was about to reveal himself as not being at one with the rest of the Sanhedrin and he couldn't foresee the consequences. The best he could hope for was that the whole matter would soon die away and his final part in it be forgotten. And even if that were not to be the case, he had wound himself up to stand and be counted and was determined to go through with it.

"Yes?" snapped Pilate, feeling irritated and ready for more trouble.

"It is nothing Sir," said Joseph, "nothing that will cause a problem to you. I beg leave to take the body of Jesus down from the cross and be responsible for the burial."

This shocked Pilate on several levels. The first was purely practical.

"He is dead? Already? Surely not; it is not enough hours." Having despatched his guards to check earlier, he had never bothered to ask for the answer.

"He is dead Sir, I assure you."

Pilate was not ready to take this information without checking. "Guard -" he called.

A guard stood forward.

"The man Jesus who was crucified earlier today. Is he dead already?"

"I do not know Sire but I will find out immediately."

A centurion was despatched to Golgotha while Pilate retired from the public chambers and Joseph was left to his own thoughts.

It did not take long. They reassembled and the centurion assured Pilate that Jesus was indeed dead. "They did not even have to break his legs, Sire, he died within three hours."

The centurion was dismissed and Pilate looked at Joseph speculatively. "And why would you want to do this?" he asked.

Joseph took comfort from the knowledge that Pilate had been

against the conviction too. But it was difficult; Joseph did not want to antagonise Pilate for suggesting he had not been strong enough.

"Sir, I do not believe this should have been brought to a trial. I think some of my people have been over zealous. I feel it is right that someone should seek a decent end to this matter."

"And that someone is you? Why should that be?"

Joseph had little answer except that he wanted to try to repair an injustice. And since Pilate had ultimately been responsible for that injustice by virtue of his position, Joseph had to give a delicate reply.

"I have long been a follower of this man but I knew how our Scribes and elders were looking upon him. I would have been just one man against the leaders. At least now I can do something for my own sake and to compensate."

"So you were a coward?"

This seemed rather unfair, thought Joseph, since Pilate could easily have been accused of the same when he had ducked the responsibility for the decision he made. Wisely, he simply bowed his head and then added one other detail.

"He is also my cousin." It might have been cleverer if he had announced this at the outset. Pilate was astonished at the news; he had no idea of the connection – which indeed Joseph had always rather kept to himself – but it would certainly explain Joseph's interest. It was quite enough for Pilate.

"Take him," said Pilate brusquely. "Bury him how you will."

Secretly he was relieved. At last someone would take the whole problem away. He had had visions of a backlash; an uprising among the more militant of the Jews against the decisions of the court and the putting to death of a preacher who was still popular among the people, if not among their leaders.

Joseph bowed his thanks and left Pilate's palace.

In fact Joseph was not the only member of the Sanhedrin who had not approved of its actions. Nicodemus, another rich Jew, had felt similarly and now he and Joseph joined forces.

Joseph had a plan. Some time earlier, and with nothing like this in mind, he had had a tomb hewn out of rock. If asked he would have said it was for himself one day in the future, but now he had a new use for it. It had never been occupied and was thus perfect for this occasion.

Together he and Nicodemus performed the sad and gruesome task of taking Jesus's body down from the cross and transporting it to the tomb nearby.

It was by now night and somehow Nicodemus had collected an enormous weight – about a hundred pounds worth – of spices. This, together with a new robe, he managed to get to the tomb. The body was wrapped in the clean robe and anointed with the mixture of myrrh and aloes.

It would be normal Jewish practice now to leave the body in its safe home until the flesh disintegrated. At some later date the bones would be collected and placed into a box and then kept for evermore in a family grave or tomb.

Their job done, Joseph and Nicodemus had one last duty to perform. The body had to be protected both from foxes and hyenas who would regard it as a delicacy waiting to be taken, and also from the body snatchers.

The workmen had done their job thoroughly however, and had left a large stone nearby ready to be rolled across the opening. It was immensely heavy and it took all their strength to move into position. This done, Joseph and Nicodemus looked at each other and knew they had done something to salve their consciences. It was a paradox that, after the senior Jews in council had caused Jesus to be put to death, it was nevertheless two particular senior Jews who took him from the cross and laid him to rest.

Joseph and Nicodemus left, satisfied with their work and their conscience a little clear.

But unknown to them, they had had an audience.

The women who had grieved and who had been wondering what to do about the body of Jesus, had been watching. Uncertain at first whether to be relieved or horrified at what was going on before their eyes, they now realised that their Son of Galilee was safe and the problem taken care of.

Satisfied there was nothing further they could do, the women went back to where they were staying and prepared for the following day, the Sabbath, when they would return with their own spices to anoint the body further.

But yet another act in the drama was being played out even as the women found their way back to their lodgings. The Chief Priests and Pharisees had had time to reflect and a thought had occurred to them.

They returned to Pilate's palace and asked to see him.

Pilate's automatic response was one of irritation. There seemed to be no end to this business. Just when he thought it was all over – the debate concluded, the prisoner crucified, the body taken care of – back they came again, no doubt with some further problem that had been eating away at them.

But he had a duty. "Let them come in," he said wearily and sat waiting.

The Chief Priests and the elders filed in and surrounded him. "Sir," said the man they had appointed negotiator, "we have remembered something that Jesus had said. Amid his claims to be the Son of God, he said that after three days he would rise again."

"I remember."

"Sir, we cannot allow the risk. Think what could happen. His disciples could go to the tomb in the night, remove the body, and then claim he was right: he *had* risen from the dead. He *must* be the Son of God."

"So?" asked Pilate, tired with this never-ending dialogue and failing to listen very carefully.

"So – this would give them the chance to pretend they had proof. You cannot trust these people. They would do anything to prove they were right and that this deceiver really is the King of the Jews. You must see Sir, we cannot take that risk."

Pilate stared round the room. Was it a reasonable argument? Or just one more example of the tiresome Jewish leaders worrying away at the problem like a dog with a bone?

While he was thinking about it, another of the Pharisees spoke. "If we do not take action to prevent this, this could prove a worse problem than the first. Claiming he was the Son of God was bad enough. But to be able to *prove* it..." He left the rest of the sentence unsaid.

Pilate came to a conclusion. It was a reasonable argument, but again he was not going to let it become his responsibility.

"So be it. But this should be your task. You can mount a watch. You have the people. Do it yourselves. And be sure to make it secure – really secure."

At least they had permission, if not Pilate's soldiers to provide the guard.

They did as he said, sending some of their Temple guards to sit by the tomb so that there was no chance of the stone – or the body – being moved.

Early the following morning, the day after the Sabbath, as the sun rose Mary Magdalene, Mary the mother of James, and Salome went back to the tomb with their own spices, to anoint the body of Jesus for themselves.

As they approached they worried about how they could move the stone. They had seen how Joseph and Nicodemus had struggled to get it into position and saw it roll down into place, resting against the side of the opening. It seemed unlikely that the three of them would have the strength to roll it away again. They would have to find some help from somewhere.

But then, in a day that was to be full of surprises, came the first.

As they approached the tomb they thought their eyes were deceiving them. The stone was not there; or rather, it had been rolled away from the entrance. The women clutched each other in alarm. They stood a few yards off, not able to bring themselves to go any closer.

Then, "Look…" cried Salome, pointing across the front of the tomb. Lying on the ground were three men dressed in the uniform of the Temple guard. They were either asleep or dead.

The women were by now petrified. They hadn't known about the conversation between Pilate and the elders and had no idea that sentries had been despatched to guard the tomb. They looked at each other, held each other tight in fear and only slowly could bring themselves to look again at the scene before them.

"Come, we must see…" said Mary Magdalene, fearfully stepping forward towards the tomb. Slowly the three of them inched their way forwards, trying not to look at the guards lying on the ground, eyes only for the blackness inside the tomb.

At the entrance, they stopped again, straining as their eyes tried to pierce the dark within.

At first they thought there was nothing there. The body of Jesus had gone, and in the darkness the tomb seemed completely empty. But as their eyes grew accustomed to the gloom they could see that the linen garments in which he had been wrapped remained, lying in a heap on the ground. The napkin, which had been bound around his head, was lying separate.

If asked, each of the three women would have different memories of what happened next. All were faint with shock and it could be no surprise that their accounts would vary, or even seem unbelievable.

According to one, she suddenly made out within the dark tomb the shape of a young man, dressed in bright white robes sitting on a small rock on the right hand side within the tomb.

The second of the women, Mary the mother of James, would swear that there were two men, also in white clothes, but this time standing.

The third woman was not sure what she witnessed. Faint, she said afterwards she had had a vision – and she couldn't remember exactly when this was – of a similar young man who had actually rolled the stone away by himself. And his appearance and action had so frightened the guards that they had all fainted away.

All three were sure however that the man, or men, or angels even, had spoken to them. Again they had different memories of the words spoken.

"Do not be afraid," one was sure she had heard. "I know you are looking for Jesus who was crucified. But he is not here; he is risen. Come – see the place where your Lord lay. And then go; go to his disciples and tell them that he is risen from the dead. Tell them that he has gone before you to Galilee and there you will all find him."

Another remembered the words: "Why are you looking for the living among the dead? He is not here; he is risen. Do you not remember what he said to you in Galilee? He prophesied that the Son of man would be delivered into the hands of sinful men and be crucified. And then *the third day he would rise again*. It is the third day now…"

Mary the mother of James was standing crying. She was sure there were two men. They asked why she was crying. "Because they have taken away my Lord and I do not know where they have laid him."

But whatever they believed they had heard or seen, what was beyond question was that the body of Jesus was not there in the tomb. And the suggestion that they should go and tell the disciples seemed the inevitable thing to do.

They hurried to where they knew the disciples were staying, saying nothing to anyone as they ran. Quickly they found them and told they what had happened. Not just that the body of Jesus was gone, but that they had been told things by people they were now coming to believe must have been angels.

Most of the disciples, who had been overwhelmed by what had happened to the man they had followed for so long and had, to their later shame, stayed away from the crucifixion, found the story difficult to believe. Peter and John alone took action. Shocked and astonished by what they had heard, they ran as fast as they could back to the tomb. John arrived first, stooped down to look in, finding it empty as the women had said. Frightened, he waited for Peter before going in.

Peter arrived a moment or two later and without hesitation strode inside. As the women had said, all that was there were the linen clothes strewn across the ground. Then John followed inside. He looked around the tomb, saw what the others had seen. If he had been in any doubt like the other disciples, he now believed beyond question. This had been the Son of God. And as the scriptures had said, and he had taught, he was now arising again.

They went back outside and looked around. The guards had apparently come back to life again and disappeared. Not knowing what else to do, the two disciples, together with Mary the mother of James and Salome, went back to where they were staying, their minds bursting with emotion and questions.

Only Mary Magdalene remained where she was.

CHAPTER 13

THE ROAD TO EMMAUS

When the three Temple guards came to life again and recovered their wits they did not know what to do.

Basically they had failed in their duty. Sent to guard the tomb, which looked safe enough anyway with the huge stone in front of it, somehow while they slept (which they shouldn't have) someone had managed to roll away the stone and steal the body within. They were only grateful it was to the Chief Priests and elders they were responsible, not the Romans. There would have been only one outcome if they had failed the Romans: death.

As soon as they woke up and realised what had happened their automatic response was to run away. The arrival of the three women must have disturbed their sleep; as they sat up they could hear the women's voices inside the tomb. Wasting no time they scrambled to their feet and rushed out of sight as fast as they could.

Once away from Golgatha they stopped to catch their breath and decide whether to be honest and tell the elders what had happened or pursue the easiest and safest course and run away.

They decided to be honest.

But it caused a huge debate among the priests and Scribes, who sent the guard out of the room while they talked. What had happened was exactly what they wanted to avoid. Now Jesus's followers could claim that their master had indeed risen from the dead, just as prophesied, and therefore really was the Son of God.

They could not leave it. After all they had caused to be done, their meetings with Pilate and Herod Antipas, and the final outcome, they could not allow all that work to be undone. After much consultation among themselves they decided on their course of action, although not all of them were in full agreement.

They called the three guards in.

The spokesman for the elders looked the guards squarely in the eyes and said, "This is what you must say: his disciples came during the night and stole him away while you were asleep. Is that completely clear? It makes you look very poor soldiers but you will have to live with that; it is your own fault after all. This is what has got to happen; we cannot risk anything else".

Two of the guards, looking sheepish, agreed. But the third, more aware of the possible consequences than the others, had a thought of his own. And it made him unexpectedly bold. He sounded almost truculent.

"Why should we do this? Why should we perjure ourselves? There is no benefit to us, only the worry of having lied."

The elders had guessed this might happen, and had their plans ready. The first was simple and would cost them nothing.

"There certainly is a benefit to you. You keep your jobs. In any other circumstances you would have been dismissed immediately. Think on that and be thankful you are still in our employ."

The third guard looked smug. He had realised they had real trump cards in their hand. If his bosses wanted something so much, there has to be a price.

He shook his head. "Not enough," he said. "In any case we can easily get other guard jobs. We require more than just an offer to keep the jobs we have got."

The elders had not really expected to get away with it, and had their second offer ready.

"We will give you money so that you can go away and live comfortably somewhere else and not have to worry."

The guard knew he had the upper hand and pushed his argument even further.

"But Pilate's men. They will find out, you know how clever they are and how determined. If Pilate thinks something is not quite right he will pursue it until he gets to the truth."

"Do not worry; we will persuade him there is nothing amiss here. We will protect you, be reassured."

The guard did not wish to be reassured and continued to look deliberately doubtful.

The elders sighed and the leader spoke again. "All right. We will give you a lot of money. What do you say now?"

The first two guards looked at the third with something approaching idolatry and then at each other and nodded. A potential disaster had been turned into a pot of gold. *And* the Chief

Priests and scribes were not compromised. There could hardly be a better outcome.

Mary Magdalene had remained at the tomb when Peter, John, Salome and Mary the mother of James had gone back to the disciples. She could not tear herself away from the place where she had last seen her Lord. She stood still for many minutes, facing towards the tomb, the tears running down her face.

But she could not stand there forever and eventually she turned to walk away, to follow the others back to the disciples.

Rather to her surprise she found a man standing near; she had not heard him arrive.

"Woman, why are you crying? Who are you looking for?" he asked gently.

Grieving as she was she did not raise her eyes to his, but concluded he must be the gardener, perhaps in charge of the land there, perhaps responsible for what had happened.

Still not looking up, she asked, "Sir, if you have taken him away, tell me where you have lain him, and I will arrange for him to be taken and looked after".

But she received no answer to this.

A strange feeling began to overtake her. In the shock of the discovery of the empty tomb she was not certain what was real and what was just in her mind.

What she thought she was hearing instead of an answer was just one word. "Mary."

Now she did raise her eyes to him. His face was both familiar and unfamiliar. Was this the gardener she was looking at? Or was he much more than that? Was he... her Lord Jesus, risen again as he had always said he would? Was she the first to see him after the crucifixion? Or was this all a dream, only his strong presence remaining in the last spot she had seen him? He was still alive in her mind. Perhaps he was alive again in real life. She wanted to believe it, and found herself answering, "Rabboni". *Master.*

The words continued, but whether they were in her mind or in reality she would never know.

He said, "Do not touch me, for I have not yet gone to my father.

Go to my brothers and disciples and tell them that I will ascend to my father and your father, to my God and your God".

The man turned and walked away, a message given.

After a moment's hesitation, Mary ran as fast as she could back to the disciples and told them what she had experienced. Excited and out of breath she had difficulty in getting the words out. For their part, they were still trying to come to terms with the crucifixion – and their own ignoble part in it. Trying to comfort themselves, they were not ready to believe the miracle of rebirth had really happened. Not yet.

However convinced Mary Magdalene was, the disciples found it too hard and could not bring themselves to believe. They needed more proof than one report from one woman. It was simply too much.

Later that day two of the disciples, Cleopas the son of Mary and Matthew the tax collector were making their way the seven and a half miles from Jerusalem to Emmaus. They were walking almost in a dream, so dramatic were the events they had just been experiencing.

They were certain of little; only that their leader, Jesus, had been put to death by order of the Romans, egged on by the requests of the Jewish priests and elders. They hardly knew what to think. The Jesus, the Messiah, they had awaited for so long had been – and gone. With so little achieved, it seemed. And yet they had loved him and were lost without him.

Was he really the Messiah? Surely he was supposed to lead the Jews out of the tyranny of the Romans and set them back on the path of self-government? And yet what had happened? He had been hung on a cross to die and the Jews were no farther forward.

Speech between the two of them was sporadic. Neither really knew what to say and they were largely concerned with their own thoughts. From time to time one of them would speak, but with little to say. They went over the ground again and found they were getting nowhere.

After a while a third man joined them, heavily veiled. There was something familiar about him, but absorbed with their own thoughts, neither really looked at him and certainly not enough to recognise what was visible of his face.

At first they just walked along together, as travellers did when they found themselves going in the same direction. But the stranger could tell there was something wrong and after a few minutes he asked them a direct question.

"Whatever have you been discussing that makes you so sad?"

Cleopas answered, "You must be a stranger in Jerusalem not to know the things that been going on these past few days."

"What things?"

The other disciple Matthew was incredulous. "What things?"

The stranger only smiled, waiting for his question to be answered.

"Jesus of Nazareth. You've heard of him, I suppose? The great prophet, mighty in deed and word before God and all the people?"

Still the stranger made no reply, but continued to look questioningly at the two disciples. Still occupied with their own thoughts, neither looked back, but Cleopas slowly outlined the story.

"The Chief Priests and the rulers of we Jews got the Roman governor to condemn him to death. He was crucified three days ago."

"Three days ago. I can understand that you should be sad, but you seem confused too. Am I right? Is everything not as it should be?"

There was a silence for a moment, as the disciples realised that somehow this stranger had penetrated their thoughts and understood something of their disappointment.

Matthew responded slowly, as though he were thinking it out as he went along. "You are right. We had believed that he was to deliver us from the Romans, that he should have led Israel so we could regain our own authority again. And yet despite his death, nothing is changed."

Then Cleopas joined in, feeling the need to share everything with this stranger now that the other disciples had told so much. Besides, this man seemed sympathetic.

"There is something else. Something we cannot explain. It is three days since our Lord Jesus was crucified and something very strange has happened. Some of the women in our group went to the tomb on the day after and what they found has astonished and alarmed us."

Matthew joined in. "The tomb was empty. The body of Jesus was gone; only some of the clothes remaining. But just as amazing, they claim they had seen… angels." He delayed saying the word, showing how hard he found it to believe. "The… angels… said he was *alive!*"

He looked at the stranger, expecting a look of disbelief on his face, but the stranger's face was curiously unresponsive, as though he knew better but could not bring himself to say.

Cleopas took up the story, growing in enthusiasm as he realised the stranger was taking it all in and not suggesting they were foolish even to be talking about it. "So some of us ran back to the tomb to see what was really going on; we thought the women in their grief must have been mistaken. But they were absolutely right. The body of our Lord Jesus was not there. The tomb was completely empty other than the few clothes scattered around."

Both disciples waited for the stranger's reaction. They had told their story and now felt a little sheepish because it made so little sense.

This time he did reply. And when he did so, it was not at all what they had expected. Far from implying that the whole story was so far-fetched that they could be forgiven for being confused, this apparently mild-mannered man now spoke to them almost sharply, in a voice quite different from that he had used earlier. The two disciples stopped short in surprise.

"Oh you people, you foolish people. Why are you so slow to believe what was prophesied in the scriptures? Didn't the prophets say that the Messiah would have to suffer like this before he could enter into his true glory?"

The two disciples stopped walking for a moment and stared into the stranger's face. It was a face that they knew and yet did not know, like a long-lost brother of a well-known friend.

The stranger started talking again and slowly they picked up their pace. There was something about the stranger's voice that held their attention to the exclusion of everything else. He obviously had a deep knowledge of the old testaments and the words of the prophets. He held them spellbound as he took them back as far as Moses and opened their eyes to all that was forecast about the coming of Jesus himself.

Before they knew it they had arrived at the end of their journey at the village of Emmaus. The stranger had clearly not finished his journey, for as they stopped he walked on, bidding them farewell.

But they were not ready to lose him. They had felt that they had spoken with a man who understood them and appreciated what they were going through. More than that even; he had helped restore their faith and encouraged them by showing how all that had passed was exactly as it *should* come to pass.

So they said, "Please stay with us. It is getting on for evening and this is no time to continue travelling. Stay and eat with us." He nodded, as though he had somehow been expecting the invitation, and entered the inn where they were staying.

They ordered a modest meal; the days recently had been so full of intensity and emotion that none of them – despite the long walk – had a great deal of appetite. As they sat, somehow the stranger had taken the head of the table, and when it was time to offer a prayer, it was the stranger who did so. Neither of the disciples minded; neither was surprised.

He took the bread, broke it, blessed it, handed it to them.

As they ate they looked at him with searching eyes; they knew him, yet they did not.

Slowly thoughts began to dawn in their minds. Neither spoke yet, each wrestling with his own ideas. And then, suddenly, they knew.

Or thought they did.

They turned away from the stranger, to look at each other. Each was about to speak; but first they found themselves wrapped in prayer. Their eyes tightly closed and thoughts racing through their minds, neither realised that the stranger had left the room. When they opened their eyes and saw the empty place at the head of the table, they said nothing for a moment, then both started to speak at once.

Cleopas said, "You know who that was?"

Matthew said, "I know who I think it was."

Cleopas, to Matthew's great surprise: "James."

Matthew: "James, the brother of Jesus?"

Cleopas: "That's why he seemed so familiar. We hardly know him, but there's a good family resemblance, do you not think?"

The thought was not the one that Matthew was having, but he stopped to consider it. It was true, they did not know James well. He had never – so far – been in the forefront of Jesus's followers. And yes, there was a family resemblance. It made sense. It could have been James, although why he had left so suddenly and quietly he could not guess.

But the problem with this theory was that it did not fit with his own. The prophets had said Jesus would rise again after three days. It was now three days. *Was this Jesus?* True, he did not look exactly like Jesus, though there was a familiarity there. On the other hand, it was hardly surprising that he was changed. Think what he had been through.

The two of them stared at each other in silence, then at the empty place at the head of the table. Slowly, mystically even, Cleopas's thoughts began to join with Matthew's. Together they began to believe.

Cleopas was the first to speak. "I know what you are thinking. I understand. When I think how our hearts were warming at the words he said to us on the journey, how he explained the scriptures in a way I have never heard before…then…there is only one person it could have been."

The other nodded in silence. It was almost too much to come to terms with.

Then they both knew they had to get back to Jerusalem to share this news with the others. Within the hour they were on the road again, dark as it was.

But when they arrived, full of their story, there was a surprise in store.

Several of the disciples were gathered together along with a number of other followers of Jesus. And before Cleopas and Matthew could tell what had happened to them, the small crowd had news for them. Amazing news. "The Lord has appeared to Peter. He says he is risen."

The two of them looked across at Peter, who simply nodded. How and when, Peter had not explained; he had simply asserted that Jesus had appeared to him and that he believed their master had indeed risen again.

Cleopas and Matthew sensed that despite the prophecies the room was not convinced by this. But they had news of their own and they blurted out their own story and how they had finally agreed, at the breaking of the bread, that Jesus had really been with them.

Yet even this was not enough to persuade everyone. They all wanted to believe, yet it was asking so much. Jesus was dead; they had seen him on the cross. Could he *really* rise again and be appearing to them like a normal person? Confused, they departed the room, agreeing to meet for a meal in the evening in a secret place, for they were all still worried about their leaders and elders and had no desire for any further skirmishes with them, particularly when they did not know what to believe themselves.

CHAPTER 14

"CAST YOUR NETS"

Behind closed doors eleven of the disciples gathered secretly for their evening meal on the first day of the week. Secretly, because they were still frightened of their Jewish leaders.

The chatter was subdued; they had too much to think about. And yet there was some relief in the room too. For the first time since their leader had been crucified they were all together, doing something normal like taking their regular evening meal together. Slowly a sense of peace descended upon them. The questions of the day were put out of their mind. However certain they were that their lord had risen again when he was with them, as soon as they were alone the doubting started again. It was easier not to think about it.

They broke their bread, said their prayers, and slowly lapsed into silence. Each was pursuing his own dream, yet each seemed to be sharing the experience. And when the experience came they all felt it as one.

Their words had petered out. And suddenly he was there in the room with them. Their reaction was not surprising: they were quite simply terrified. In his own mind, each was sure he was looking at a ghost.

Reading their minds was not difficult and Jesus spoke to them quietly. "Peace be with you."

They made no reply, fear and awe stilling their words.

"Why are you so troubled? What are these thoughts you are having? Do you think I am a spirit?"

Still they could not answer. None of them could quite believe what was happening. Some thought they were having a personal daydream that the others were not sharing. Some felt that they were seeing what they wanted to see, rather than what was actually happening. Some, slowly, began to believe again that the scriptures were indeed being fulfilled and that their saviour had indeed risen from the dead.

He stood before them and although it disappointed him, knew they needed some proof. They were human.

"Look at my hands. Look at my feet. You can see: it is me. You can touch me and that will tell you. A spirit has no flesh or bones as I have." And he held out his hands to them and showed his feet. The wounds were visible; there should be no doubt.

But they still could not bring themselves to believe wholeheartedly. Part of each of them was bursting with joy; part was overwhelmed with fear that it was not true. That they were dreaming it all. And perhaps they were, although it did not matter, since if they believed it, in a way it was true.

Jesus watched while they wrestled with their thoughts and wanted to spur them on. He spoke strongly: "I am sad that you do not believe. That you did not believe what you have already been told, that I am indeed alive. Your hearts are hard rather than warm, your minds are not accepting that which they should accept."

The disciples looked sheepish. He had read their thoughts and they were ashamed.

As he watched their faces he knew it was time he helped them again. "You have food here," he said. "Give me some meat."

They passed him some broiled fish on a plate and a honeycomb. He took it from them and ate.

And then he said, "Do you remember the words I spoke to you when I was with you before? That everything must be done as it was written in the laws of Moses and in the prophets and in the psalms, concerning me?" As he looked round at their faces, he saw understanding beginning to dawn. Yes, the scriptures *were* being fulfilled. Yes, they had the right to believe. Yes, they could let their joy take over their souls.

But he had not finished. He wanted to make it so clear there could be no misunderstanding and no doubting. "This is how it is written: that the Christ would suffer and rise from the dead on the third day. That repentance and forgiveness of sins should be preached in his name all over the lands, beginning here in Jerusalem. And you are all witnesses of these things."

After these words he was silent, fixing them all with that compelling stare he had, that look from which there was no escape, and which always meant he was asking something of them. The disciples were spellbound, going over his words again in their minds, beginning to realise that this was a moment that would change their lives for ever, that they were being charged with the biggest task imaginable.

He continued. "As my father sent me, now I send you. Go forth from this house – but first wait in Jerusalem until you are given the power from above. Then go into the world and preach the gospel to every man and woman. And everyone of those who hears and believes and is baptised will be saved. They will speak with a new tongue and cast out the devils. Serpents and poison will not hurt them. And if they lay their hands on the sick they will be healed. But if they do *not* believe, they will be condemned to eternal damnation." Not mincing his words, he was as strong as ever.

Still they were silent, each trying to comprehend the enormity of what he was saying, and what he was demanding they should do. That he was no longer the leader, but that they should all become leaders.

Then, finally, the most awe-inspiring words of all. "Receive the gift of the Holy Ghost. Whosoever sins you forgive, they shall be forgiven. Repentance and forgiveness of sins must be preached through all nations. But those sins you do *not* forgive, they shall be their burden for evermore. You have witnessed what I have said, you know what is to be done."

The disciples looked at each other, trying to take in just what was being asked of them. And then, when they looked back, just as with Cleopas and Matthew, he was gone.

There was one disciple who had been absent throughout all of this: Thomas, who was also known as Didymus (the ancient name for a twin). When the others found him they wasted no time in telling him what he had missed.

"We have seen the Lord! He has appeared to us." They were so buoyed up with excitement that the prophecies had been fulfilled and that their beloved master was again with them that it never occurred to them to consider what a difficult thing it would be for someone who had not been there to comprehend.

They expected delight; they received a blank face.

"I cannot believe it. It cannot be possible." He was stubborn.

"Unless I see the print of the nails in his hands and put my fingers into those prints and push my hand into his side where the spear pierced him, I cannot believe."

The disciples were shocked, though they were able to recall their own difficulties in believing, realising that it was only because they were actually in the room with him that they themselves were able to believe. And however much they tried to reason with Thomas and persuade him by recounting exactly what had happened, he refused to accept it.

Until a week later when the disciples were gathered again in the room where they had been when they had last seen their master. This time Thomas was with them.

The doors were closed, but suddenly they realised that Jesus was there, saying, as he had before, "Peace be with you".

Then he addressed Thomas directly. "Put your fingers here, feel my hand. Put your hand here into my side. Believe - and let your faith be strong again."

Thomas did as he was commanded. Fearfully he touched Jesus, careful so that he did not hurt him, guilty that he had doubted. All were silent for a moment, until Thomas, overwhelmed and distraught that he had ever questioned and barely able to look Jesus in the eye, said simply, "My Lord and my God".

Jesus looked back and said, "Thomas - because you have seen me you have believed. But even more blessed are those who have not seen me but still believed."

Thomas cast his eyes downwards at the rebuke. And when he looked up again, only the disciples remained in the room.

They tried to return to some sort of normality. There were no more appearances and the disciples started to pick up their lives again. On the outside they could manage the usual day-to-day things that were necessary, but inside they were still in anguish at the loss of their leader.

Also they did not know what to do. They had been suddenly cut adrift. A boat without a rudder.

They idled about, spending much time praying for guidance, but with no success. Trying to lift himself out of this lethargy, one day Peter said to some of them, "I think I'll go fishing. Who wants to come with me?"

Several of them did: Thomas the twin - now determined to stay with them in every way, Nathaniel from Cana, James and John the sons of Zebedee, Matthias (who had replaced Judas among the disciples) and Bartholomew.

There was a small boat they often used and in the early evening they set sail on the Sea of Galilee. Several of the other disciples also set sail in a second boat. After the days of doing little it was satisfying to be taking some action at last and they all began to feel a little more like themselves again. They were cheerful as they cast off; pleased to be taking their minds off the events of the last few weeks, looking forward to a little sport, mixed with the real benefit of finding fresh food for themselves.

But it was not to be. It was a very quiet night, and the sails of the boat hardly filled. They drifted a few hundred feet off shore, cast out their nets - and caught nothing. The second boat did no better.

Several times they lifted the anchor, sailed a little further on, cast the nets again. And the nets stayed stubbornly empty. As the new day dawned, grey and unfriendly, they looked at each other and decided it was time to return to the shore. Their trip, on which they had set out with such good humour and anticipation, had proved fruitless.

There was a mist over the water and as they came closer to the shore they noticed the figure of a man standing there, watching. It was too far and too misty to make anything out - not even whether he was young or old, rich or poor.

But his words carried clearly through the fresh morning air: "Friends - have you caught anything?"

"No," they answered together and with feeling, "not a thing."

"Try the other side," the figure called back, "cast the net on the right side of the boat and you'll find plenty."

It was not usual to do this. Traditionally the nets were on the left and the boat went around it in a circle.

But they had nothing to lose. Rather dispiritedly - irritated, even, that someone they did not know presumed to tell them how to work their nets and go against the time-honoured system, Nathaniel and

James, with a rather reluctant Matthias lending a disinterested hand, transferred the nets across the boat to the right hand side and cast them into the water.

Some of the disciples stared down into the water. They expected nothing. And they were completely wrong. To their amazement the water started to swirl and eddy and they could see beneath the surface the movement of fish. All the more amazing since they had not seen one fish all night. As the light and mist continued to clear, they stared in astonishment. All off them crossed to the right side of the boat, causing it to list alarmingly. But it was to do more than that, for as the nets quickly filled up and pulled at the boat it leaned over still farther.

"Move across," called Peter to the others, "or we'll be over." Obediently the disciples returned to the left hand side of the boat and it regained some of its balance. Now that everything had changed so totally they hardly knew what to do. In place of the empty, flapping nets, there was now the complete opposite: nets so full they could not draw them aboard and hardly keep the boat upright.

Slowly they made their way towards the shore, hoping to get to the shallow waters before the boat capsized. They had known nothing like it and at the back of their minds some began to wonder.

One did more than wonder. John – always the closest to Jesus – had come to a conclusion: this was Jesus appearing to the disciples yet again. John drew Peter aside and whispered, "It is the Lord". Peter stared abruptly back at the figure on the shore. He could still not see properly but knew there was one thing he had to do quickly, just in case. Fishing is a very wet business, and Peter, in common with some of the others, had stripped himself of his clothes while he worked. His first thought – if this indeed was Jesus – was that he must make himself presentable again, and quickly drew on his dry tunic.

This done, he immediately soaked it, for he threw himself into the water and started to swim ashore.

The second boat was about two or three hundred feet behind. Too distant to hear the instructions from the shore, they had watched while the first boat had switched its nets from side to side, and did the same. And like the first boat, they too filled their nets.

The two boats got as far inland as they could with their full nets.

When the keels struck the thick sand, all stopped and jumped into the water.

Slowly and with difficulty they dragged their overflowing nets onto the shore one at a time, returning to the boats for more.

But when they had finished and all the nets were ashore and they came out of the water themselves, they were astonished to find a great fire of coals already alight, some fish roasting over the heat, and bread ready to accompany the meal.

The disciples tried to look at the figure they had seen on the shore without staring. Now that he was only yards from them, in their minds they were sure it must be Jesus, even though they could not exactly recognise him. Yet none of them dared to ask in case they would be accused of not believing – or perhaps that they had got it wrong and they were seeing what they wanted to see. Yet instinctively they knew they *must* believe, and from then on they acted as though they could take it for granted and it was their Lord appearing to them again.

He said, "Bring the fish you have caught up here".

Peter went down to the shore and dragged a net up towards the fire. The net was near bursting with over a hundred and fifty large fish, yet somehow it did not break, despite being hauled over the rough shore.

Jesus then said to them, "Come – eat". They walked forward, still a little unsure in their minds, even though their hearts were telling them this was indeed Jesus.

As they approached, Jesus took the fish and bread and gave it to them, reminding them all of the last supper they had had together. Together on the shore they ate. But there was not much talk; the disciples were too overwhelmed to maintain anything like a normal conversation. And Jesus? He could see their difficulties, understood them, tried to talk easily with them but knew nothing was normal any more. Besides, he had something else on his mind.

When they had finished their breakfast, Jesus fixed his eyes on Peter and asked him a direct question.

"Peter, son of Jonas, do you love me more than these?" He pointed to the other disciples there, but Peter instinctively knew he meant not just those on the shore, but every man who lived.

Peter replied, "Yes, of course my Lord – you know I love you." He could not understand the question. The words "Of course" were the most natural in the world for him to say.

But Jesus was not finished; this was the beginning of Peter's battle orders, and he was going to filter them in gently. The reply from Jesus when it came was slow and rather mystical.

"Feed my lambs."

The question came again. "Peter, son of Jonas, do you love me?" Peter could only make the same reply: "You know that I love you". He was puzzled. What else could he say? And why was he being asked twice?

Jesus's reply did not help to answer his wonder. "Then care for my sheep."

Peter nodded. He did not really understand, but then he had frequently not understood what Jesus was saying; he just knew that Jesus was always right and that it was his duty and even privilege just to follow where his master led.

But still Jesus had not finished. Again he asked the question, now for the third time, "Peter – do you love me?"

Peter was sad. Sad that his Lord had felt the need to ask him the same question three times, as though he were not satisfied with the answer – or worse, did not believe it. There was a touch of exasperation mixed with disappointment in Peter's reply this time.

"Lord – you know everything. You *know* that I love you."

At first Jesus's response did nothing to calm Peter's unease. "Then feed my sheep," he said again.

Peter waited; there must be more. Jesus took a little while before he continued, but when he did it was not exactly to explain what he had been repeating. Instead he reverted to the Jesus of old and used his own particular way of talking. It was a sort of parable.

"When you were young you dressed as you wanted and went where you wanted."

Peter and the others looked back at their master and waited to see where this was leading.

Jesus went on, "But as you grow old you will have to stretch out your hand for help and guidance; others will dress you and take you where perhaps you do not want to go."

The disciples waited for this to be explained, for the purpose of the words were not clear to them. But Jesus said nothing further, leaving them with their own thoughts.

In the silence that followed, each worried at Jesus's words in his mind and began to realise that what he was really doing was referring to his own death. In the end he had had no chance to defend himself or make his own decisions. Events had overtaken him, and although in the end the words of the prophets had been fulfilled, it was not in the way anyone might have expected.

The words slipped their way into Peter's heart, but still he puzzled over the repetition of "Feed my sheep". He could only imagine it meant give succour to those who need it. But there was no helpful answer coming from Jesus. Instead, just two words.

"Follow me." Jesus started to move away. The words seemed to be addressed just to Peter and he started to follow Jesus. But something caught his eye, and turning round, Peter saw that John was beginning to follow too. This was the same man who had leaned across to Jesus at their last supper together and asked who would betray him.

Both had misunderstood. "Follow me" meant "Follow my teaching" and "Follow my belief". Once again the disciples had failed to see the real meaning behind Jesus's words. Peter stopped, looked back at John, and spoke to Jesus again.

"Lord - what should this man John do?"

The meaning of Jesus's answer was not clear to Peter and it led to much misunderstanding. Jesus said, "If I want him to stay alive until I return, what is that to you? Just follow me."

All the disciples heard this and took the wrong meaning from it. They talked about it later and decided Jesus had meant that John was never to die but live just as Jesus himself was living again. It was an idea that lived on as a rumour for years. Yet it was quite wrong, for Jesus had meant exactly what he had said: not that John would not die, but just that he should wait.

They were puzzled; puzzled by Jesus's words, unclear what they were supposed to do. And while they stood, uncertain, they realised that, once again, Jesus was no longer with them.

CHAPTER 15

THE HILL OF HOPE

They often used to meet in a particular place on one of the hills of Galilee. Here Jesus chose to talk to them, pray with them, instruct them. Somehow, almost without discussing it, they found themselves climbing the hill again on the morning after the fishing expedition.

None of them spoke. It was as though they all had had some secret message, spelled out by no-one but understood by them all.

When they arrived they waited in silence. If asked, each would have said the same thing: "We are waiting for Jesus; we know he will come".

And he did come, appearing without warning. There was no surprise among the disciples, no fear this time. The only question among some of them was the reality of what was happening. Most believed whole-heartedly that the Son of God had been reborn and was among them again. But a few still wondered whether it was all a figment of their imagination; that they had followed their master so devotedly for so long that their minds refused to believe he had gone; that his presence was so strong in their hearts that they could actually *see* him when they wanted to.

But while those few who were still doubting wondered, Jesus spoke to them all.

"I have been given complete power, both in heaven and here on earth. So I say to you, go out into the world and spread my word among all nations. Baptise them in the name of the Father and the Son and the Holy Ghost. Teach them all the things I have taught you. And remember, I am with you always, right until the end of the world."

Such was the force of his words that at last even the doubters put away their doubts and determined to do as he had commanded them.

But he had not finished yet. "When I was with you in the past I told you that everything that had been written by Moses and the prophets and in the psalms concerning me would come true."

The disciples stirred with the memories of the preachings of Jesus in those very hills. He had indeed said that and now it all appeared to be coming true.

He went on. "It was written long ago that the Messiah must suffer and die and rise again from the dead on the third day. It has been done as it was said. So you have my authority to take the message of repentance to all nations, beginning in Jerusalem. Everyone who follows me shall receive forgiveness for their sins. And it is *you* who must make this come about."

Now the disciples were really quiet. Many closed their eyes, contemplating the enormous responsibility Jesus had laid upon them and wondering whether they were strong enough. At the back of their minds was the fact they could never forget, that they had shamefully stayed away from the crucifixion and so in a way betrayed their leader. Now, perhaps, that sin could be forgiven, just as Jesus had said every man's sins would be forgiven if he followed the words of the saviour. Through the worry they began to feel a sense of joy.

Then, without speaking further, he led them down the hill to Bethany, where he had been staying just before his trial.

They stood silently in a semicircle, looking at him, sensing this was the most important moment in their lives.

Silently he raised his hands and blessed them. It was, they knew, the final farewell. The emotion was too strong and they wept, closing their eyes and pulling their veils down over their faces. In their minds they could see the sight they had stayed away from; their leader nailed on a cross on the hill of Golgatha, the hill where everything seemed lost.

Opening their eyes at last, they knew he would be gone. Their gaze moved upwards to where they had seen and heard him only a short time earlier, where he had filled their hearts with joy and given them their great task.

This was a different hill; a hill of hope.

CHAPTER 16

AFTERWARDS

It was the most extraordinary story.

An entire family was sitting together at supper: father, mother, two daughters, a small son, and a grandfather, Jacob.

"Tell us again, grandfather," said the son, Ahab. They already knew the story well; so they should, they had asked and been told it a dozen times. But it was so extraordinary.

Jacob smiled. He had been there and he loved telling the story. But he believed in making his audience work, especially Ahab, who would carry the story forward into the coming generations.

"All right Ahab. When did it take place?"

"At Pentecost, grandfather Jacob."

"And when was Pentecost?"

"Seven weeks after Jesus was born again."

"And what does Pentecost celebrate?"

"It's the festival of Shavuot in remembrance of God giving the ten commandments to Moses on Mount Sinai. And it's the end of the grain harvest too."

"Good boy," beamed Jacob; the son would be a good ambassador for the believers.

"So tell us again, grandfather, about all the different languages and the big wind and the tongues of fire."

"Steady boy," said Jacob, "do you want me to tell the story or do you want to do it for me?"

"Quiet Ahab," said his two elder sisters, "it's grandfather's story. He can tell it best."

The two parents exchanged smiles; they as much as the children enjoyed the story. And they knew what pleasure it gave the old man to live it again. He settled more comfortably, his tired legs propped up on a stool, a glass at his hand to moisten the throat when it became dry.

"I don't know it all, mind. I was not one of the disciples. But I know what I saw and what I was told. It was, as you say boy, seven weeks after that day when the Lord rose again. It was quite early in the morning and I was in Jerusalem with friends and we started to hear rumours, that something amazing was happening at one end of the town.

"We all hurried up there, to find ourselves part of a huge multitude, all drawn to see what was going on. It seemed that the disciples had all been gathering together for their meal when suddenly there was a sound from heaven, a sound like a rushing mighty wind and it filled the whole house and shook it…"

"Like a great tornado!" burst in Ahab, unable to control his excitement.

"Like a great tornado. But that was just the beginning…"

"The flames of fire!" Ahab could not keep quiet.

Jacob tried to ignore him. "And then, as they were sitting there, they saw fingers of fire like tongues cut in two, and the flames settled over each of them…"

"What did it look like, flames on top of the people?"

"I've told you Ahab," said Jacob wearily, "I was not there at that time. I didn't see the tongues of fire. I was just told about it."

Ahab knew it of course, but always hoped his grandfather would suddenly change his mind about his memories and suddenly recall something else. Nevertheless he went on with his questions, always hoping for a little more drama.

"And did the flames burn them?"

"No, they did not burn them. It was fire from heaven so it was holy fire and it did not burn them. It was a sign, just a sign." Ahab looked disappointed. "But it was a sign from heaven above, and nothing is more grand and more important than that. But by this time we had all got there. The doors were open and we swarmed into the house to see for ourselves just what was going on. And it was *amazing*. It was a miracle. Because the disciples must have been filled with some kind of magic from heaven, for they started to speak in all different languages. So that every one of us – and we came from all over the city and with many different backgrounds – could understand, for they were talking in all our own languages. It was completely amazing, for as we said to ourselves, these men are Galileans, they are not students and scholars of language. And yet they are talking so that we can all understand them, no matter where our families come from. Now, Ahab – and you girls – how many of the places can you remember where we all came from?"

Ahab and his two sisters started to reel off the names.

"Parthians and Medes."

"Elamites"

"People from Mesopotamia…"

"… and from Judea and Cappadocia, from Pontus and Asia."

"Cretans…"

"Arabians…"

They were slowing down now and needed a little help. Jacob prompted, "People from Egypt?"

"Yes – from Phrygia…"

"…and Pamphylia."

"And from Libya. And…" Jacob again.

There was a silence, until their mother filled in the last names. "The Cyrenians And of course people who had come from Rome and travelling Jews who were in the city."

Jacob went on, the list finished to his satisfaction. "And of course we were all amazed that they should be able to talk to us like that, in all those different languages.

But, of course, after a few minutes some people started to get suspicious. 'They're drunk – they're not talking different languages at all. It's all a joke…' But then Peter, one of the most important of the disciples stood up and shouted at them."

"And what did he say? Was he very cross with them?"

"In a way. The manner in which he spoke made them feel embarrassed. He said, 'You men of Judea and those who are staying here in Jerusalem – just listen to what I say and pay close attention to my words. First of all, these men are not drunk. It is only nine in the morning. Whoever is drunk by nine in the morning? No, this is the prophecy of Joel which has come to pass. Remember what he said…'".

But Ahab could not sit through the whole speech again, much as Jacob loved delivering it.

"Just tell us the important bits grandfather."

Jacob made a grimace over the heads of the children to their parents and went on. "Well, he said that he would pour out his spirit upon everyone. That everyone who calls on the name of the Lord for help will be saved. That God raised up Jesus and took the pain of death away and set him at his right hand. And that they should be in no doubt that this *was* Jesus, the son of God."

"So how did you all behave then, now you had heard all this from Peter?"

"Well boy, I must say that those who had laughed and said they were all drunk looked very sorry for themselves. Peter's words had been so strong and so convincing that everyone there became a true believer."

"And so what happened then?"

"Well, first of all, they felt so guilty and so persuaded that they asked Peter what they ought to do. Peter told them that they should repent and that every one of us should be baptized in the name of Jesus so that we would be forgiven our sins. Then we would receive the gift of the Holy Ghost."

"What does that mean?" Ahab knew perfectly well what it meant, but loved to hear it from the old man's lips.

"It meant that you became a different person. *You would have Jesus in your heart for all time.* You, your children, even the non-Jews – the Gentiles."

Ahab was silent at this, the thought overwhelming.

The old man had not quite finished. "The last thing that Peter said was this would help us save ourselves from those of our generation who had gone astray."

"So did they have themselves baptised?"

"You'll find this hard to believe, boy, but no less than three thousand people went for baptism. And then they began to meet in small groups, and break bread just as Jesus had done, and follow in his ways. And do you know, some of those were such believers that they sold their houses and all their possessions and gave the money and goods away to those who needed them. They worshipped at the temple every day and slowly but surely there were more and more of them. It was really the beginning of the birth of our great movement, spreading the word of Jesus and God."

"Just like you have done," said Ahab.

Old man Jacob smiled. "Just like me."

But Jacob was too optimistic. There was still huge opposition to what Jesus stood for and had been preaching. And before long the Jews who had believed in the coming of the Lord, in Jesus the Christ, were being driven underground. The senior Jews and the Roman leaders had agreed on one thing: they must prevent the followers of Jesus being as much trouble as Jesus himself had been.

There was a big movement to have all these followers driven out of Jerusalem and all the other big towns. And no-one was more determined to exterminate all of Jesus's followers than the Pharisee and Roman citizen Saul Paulos of Tarsus. He called himself the "Hebrew of Hebrews" and the only issue in his mind was the great divide between the Jewish leaders and the word of Jesus. He was devoting himself to doing everything possible to rid the country of what he still called the upstarts.

He had already "cleansed" most of Jerusalem, where in his own words he had "laid waste to the upstarts, arresting the followers of Jesus and having them thrown into gaol".

He went to Ciaiphas, the High Priest, who was delighted to have found such a soldier in the cause. Saul was intelligent, strong, well-educated, determined. Ciaiphas provided him with a small army of soldiers and a bundle of letters, officially imprinted with the seal of his office and the full authority of the Sanhedrin, addressed to all synagogues and admonishing them to provide all the aid Saul might need. The letters also gave him power to arrest all followers of Jesus of Nazareth.

Saul had set himself the task of travelling north to the beginning of the desert and of tracking down every one of these new Christians he could find. He promised to bring them all back to Jerusalem in chains for imprisonment and probable execution.

He set off with his cavalry full of anticipation. But strangely he found no-one. Travelling in the general direction of Damascus in Syria he could not understand why there was not a single Christian to be found; no meetings, no clusters in doorways, no information to be gleaned from anyone.

Until he came to the outskirts of Damascus. It was a place of two rivers, with the city lying between them. The fields were fertile and verdant and the yearly harvest rich.

He and his personal army were tired and thirsty after their journey over the dusty roads. He knew the city and was looking forward to a satisfying meal and a good night's rest in the main inn in the "Street that is called Straight".

They were half a mile from their destination, rest and recovery almost in sight, when Saul felt a wave of giddiness sweep over him and he swayed in the saddle of his great white horse. Suddenly a freezing wind was rushing past and around him; he could hear a sound like the rushing of great tidal waters. And then like a bolt from the sky he was surrounded by blinding white light.

Disorientated and unbalanced he grabbed at the reins to steady himself but his hands were not his own; they had no strength in them and, losing his balance totally he fell from the horse.

Almost unconscious from the fall he lay on the ground fighting for his breath and praying for the world to stop spinning.

Then, suddenly, the sounds and the wind stopped, to be replaced by a voice in his ear; a voice he could not recognise yet felt faintly familiar.

"Saul, Saul," it said, "Why do you persecute me?"

He did not know the voice but knew it was a voice of authority.

"My lord – who are you who speaks to me?"

The answer was the last he expected.

"I am Jesus, the one you persecute. But it is useless for you to kick against the pricks of the goad."

Saul was astounded and puzzled. This was *Jesus*, speaking to *him*? And what did it mean, useless to kick against the goad? A goad, as Saul knew well, was the long stick sharpened at one end used by cowmen to herd their cattle. At nine feet in length it was impossible for the cows to reach and kick back at their masters. Did this mean that however much he travelled and however many followers he captured he could never overcome Jesus and his teachings?

Lying on the ground his mind was awash with fear and confusion. And then, suddenly, out of nowhere, came a great compulsion to help.

He could only ask, "Lord, what will you have me do?"

"Get up and go into the city and there you will be told what to do."

Still Saul lay on the ground, his mind so full at first he could not bring himself to rise up. But when he did begin he found the struggle was beyond him.

His men, too, were confused, for they had heard a voice – though they could not understand what it was saying – but could see no-one.

Eventually the spell was broken and they came to Saul to help him to his feet. But when they had done so, and he was standing again, another shock awaited him, for he realised he could see nothing. He was blind.

They did not trouble to attempt to get him back on his horse, but instead led him by the hand into the city. Inside the gates they were met by a servant who had evidently been expecting them, for he led them straight away to the Street that is called Straight, and to a house there owned by a man called Judas; a man who because of his namesake had suffered much from the followers of Jesus.

Judas knew Saul's reputation but nevertheless welcomed him in and took him to a room which was specially prepared for him. But Saul had not recovered from the shocks and could not bring himself either to eat or drink.

For three days he remained in this state; still blind, taking no nourishment and losing his strength.

Meanwhile another man in Damascus was also having a vision.

One of Jesus's followers, Ananias, lived there. And while sleeping one night the lord appeared to him in a dream, calling him and tell him to get up and go to the Street that is called Straight, find the house of Judas and ask for Saul of Tarsus, who would be found praying. Further, in Saul's prayers he would have seen a vision of Ananias coming, so he would be prepared.

But Ananias was worried by this. He had heard all about Saul and knew his reputation. "Lord," he replied, " I know of this man. Many people have told me of the evil he has done to your followers in Jerusalem. Wherever he goes he has authority to condemn those who follow you and put them in chains."

But Jesus reassured him – and amazed him. "You go, nevertheless. For I have chosen this man as my instrument to bear my name before all: before the Gentiles, before the children of Israel, before kings even. And I will show him also how he must suffer for my name. But first there is a task for you. You must lay your hands upon his eyes, for he has been blind these last three days. And through you the scales will fall from his eyes and he will see again."

Ananias did exactly as asked. He went to the house of Judas, found Saul there at prayer and laid his hands on him, saying, "Saul my brother, the lord Jesus appeared to me as he did to you and sent me to give you back the power of sight, that you should be a new man and filled with the Holy Ghost".

Ananias did as Jesus had said and laid his hands on Saul's eyes and immediately his sight was returned. Straightaway he felt hunger and thirst return to him and he asked for food and drink.

A new man was, indeed, born.

Once recovered a little the first thing Saul asked was that he should be baptized, which Ananias was glad to do. This achieved he stayed a number of days there in Damascus with the believers who lived there. His rebirth was confirmed by his actions. To the amazement of all who knew his reputation, he started preaching in the synagogues there, not against Jesus but for him.

It was not easy. People could not believe it at first. "Is this not the man who fought against those who followed Jesus in Jerusalem and condemned them to gaol or death? And hasn't he come here to do exactly the same thing? To bind them in chains and take them to the Chief Priests?"

But as Saul found his strength returning, so did his preaching become stronger and the people began to believe in him and his conversion.

As a new man he began his travels.

And found some difficulties.

In Caesarea he met with the Roman King Agrippa, an expert in Jewish custom and religion. He was not ready to accept Saul's transformation without searching question. But Saul was ready with his answers and held nothing back.

And about the words spoken to him by Jesus while on the ground he was even more fulsome, perhaps adding a few words to underline the extent of his conversion.

"Get up and stand on your feet," he claimed Jesus had said to him. "I appoint you as a servant and witness. I send you to open their eyes and turn them from darkness to light, from Satan to God, so that they may receive forgiveness of sins and a place among those who have faith in me. And I will protect you in the life ever after."

Agrippa was not sure what to think. It could be said that Saul was now a traitor, having completely reversed his views and no longer being on the side of the Romans and Jewish leaders. He was uncertain what to do; so, as is often for the best in the face of uncertainty, he did nothing and allowed Saul to leave his presence, hoping he had heard the last of this apparently now unbalanced man.

But that was not to be.

The next thing that Saul did was to change his name. The name Saul was Hebrew and that was how he was known by everyone. But now he reverted to his official name as a Roman citizen: Paul.

And as Paul he travelled far and wide, spreading the word of Jesus like no man had done before him. He wrote many great letters; in one to the Corinthians he reminded them how Jesus had risen from the dead and appeared to Peter and the other disciples. That he had then appeared to a multitude of followers. And that finally, his last appearance had been to Paul himself, but, as he added, "I am the least of the apostles, who am not really worthy of the name, since I persecuted the Church of God. True, I have since worked hard, but it is the grace of God that has done it, not me."

But life was not to have a happy ending for Paul. On returning to Jerusalem after his travels he was arrested for treason by the Romans who felt, not surprisingly, that he had very publicly let them down. He was sent to Rome for trial and after two years in prison was executed under the Emperor Nero.

No-one had worked harder to spread the word. "The Road to Damascus" has been used ever since as a term to denote the biggest turning point in a man's life. But Paul had found, as so many found after him, that nothing was more difficult than to change the minds of cynics and unbelievers.

Even for something as powerful as that which was forged on a hill in Galilee.